D0075668

INTERACTIVE CHILDREN, COMMUNICATIVE TEACHING

Enriching the primary curriculum: child, teacher, context

Series editor: Janet Moyles

The series highlights some of the major challenges and issues which face teachers on a day-to-day basis in handling their apparently ever widening roles in primary schools. Curriculum experiences can, and should be enriching and stimulating for everyone but there must be a recognition and appreciation of the crucial interface between child, teacher and the context of school and society, rather than a focus on mere curriculum 'delivery'.

Each volume in the series seeks to enrich and extend readers' curriculum thinking beyond the current narrow confines through recognizing and celebrating the very essence of what makes primary teaching demanding but exciting, creative, dynamic and, yes, even enjoyable! The series recognizes that at the heart of teaching lies children and that 'subjects' are merely tools towards enabling an education which develops both understanding and enthusiasm for lifelong learning.

The authors' underpinning, integrated rationale is to enable teachers to analyse their own practices by exploring those of others through cameos of real life events taken from classroom and school contexts. The aim throughout is to help teachers regain their sense of ownership over changes to classroom and curricular practices and to develop an enhanced and enriched understanding of theory through practice.

Current and forthcoming titles:

INTERACTIVE CHILDREN, COMMUNICATIVE TEACHING
ICT and classroom teaching

Deirdre Cook and
Helen Finlayson

Open University Press
Buckingham • Philadelphia

Open University Press
Celtic Court
22 Ballmoor
Buckingham
MK18 1XW

LB
1028.46
.C686
1999

e-mail: enquiries@openup.co.uk
world wide web: http://www.openup.co.uk

and
325 Chestnut Street
Philadelphia, PA 19106, USA

First Published 1999

A catalogue record of this book is available from the British Library

ISBN   0 335 20021 4 (hb)   0 335 20020 6 (pb)

Library of Congress Cataloging-in-Publication Data
Cook, Deirdre, 1943–
    Interactive children, communicative teaching: ICT and classroom teaching/Deirdre Cook and Helen Finlayson.
        p.   cm. – (Enriching the primary curriculum – child, teacher, context)
    Includes bibliographical references (p.) and index.
    ISBN 0–335–20021–4 (hard). – ISBN 0–335–20020–6 (pbk.)
    1. Pedagogic computer applications.   2. Information and communications technology.   3. Primary education.
    I. Finlayson, Helen, 1945–   II. Title.   III. Series.
    LB1028.46.C686 1999
    371.33′4–dc21   99–12583
                                                                                      CIP

Typeset by Graphicraft Limited, Hong Kong
Printed in Great Britain by The Cromwell Press, Trowbridge

Contents

Series editor's preface

Cameo

Glenn has taught across the age range in different primary schools for the last 15 years, specializing in art. In that time, he has had to make many adjustments in his thinking. The emphasis now appears to have shifted significantly from considering the learning needs of children as paramount, to 'delivering' a curriculum over which he feels little ownership and about which he feels even less real enthusiasm! The National Curriculum, with its individual subjects and language of 'teaching', not to mention an impending Office for Standards in Education (Ofsted) inspection, has shaken his confidence somewhat in his own understanding of what primary education is all about. It has also meant that he feels *he* is doing most of the learning, rather than the children – all those detailed plans and topic packs for individual subjects which teachers have been developing within the school seem to Glenn to leave little for children to actually do except explore the occasional artefact and fill in worksheets.

Yet he knows that he enjoys the 'buzz' of teaching, revels in being part of children's progress and achievements, delights in those rare times when he can indulge in art activities with children, is appreciated by parents and colleagues for the quality of his work and, generally, still finds his real heart lies in being an educator and doing something worthwhile. His constant question to himself is 'How can I work with children in ways I feel and *know* are appropriate and yet meet the outside demands made on me?'

Sound familiar? You may well begin to recognize a 'Glenn' within you! He encapsulates the way many teachers are feeling at the present time and the persistent doubts and uncertainties which continually underpin many teachers' work. In the early and middle years of primary schooling in particular, teachers are facing great challenges in conceiving how best to accommodate the learning needs of children in a context of growing pressure, innovation and subject curriculum demand. Yet conscientiousness drives the professional to strive for greater understanding – that little bit more knowledge or skill might just make a big difference to one child, or it might provide improved insights into one aspect of the curriculum.

Glenn, like many teachers, needs time, encouragement and support to reflect on his current practice and to consider in an objective way the changes needed. Rather than trying to add something else to an already overcrowded curriculum, today's teachers should consider those existing aspects which are funda- mental to ensuring that children are not only schooled but edu- cated in the broadest possible sense. Only then can we begin to sort out those things which are vital, those things we would like to do, and those things which would benefit from a rethink.

This series aims to offer practitioners food for thought as well as practical and theoretical support in establishing, defining and refining their own understandings and beliefs. It focuses particu- larly on enriching curriculum experiences for everyone through recognizing and appreciating the crucial interface between the child, the teacher and the context of primary education, includ- ing the curriculum context. Each title in the series seeks collec- tively and individually to enhance teachers' understanding about the theories which underpin, guide and enrich quality practice in a range of broader curriculum aspects, while acknowledging issues such as class size and overload, common across primary schools today.

Each book operates from the basis of exploring teachers' sound – frequently intuitive – experiences and understanding of teach- ing and learning processes and outcomes which most teachers inevitably possess in good measure and which, like Glenn, they often feel constrained to use. For example, the editor is regularly told by teachers and others in primary schools that they 'know' or 'feel' that play for children is or must be a valuable process, yet they are also aware that this is not often reflected in their

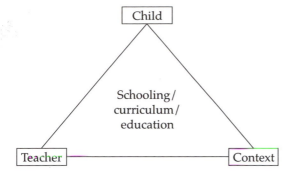

Figure 1 Child, teacher, context

planning or curriculum management and that the context of education generally is antithetical to play. What is more, they really do not know what to do about it and find articulating the justification for play practices extremely difficult. Other writers in the series have suggested that this is also the case in their areas of expertise.

All the books in this series seek to enrich and extend teachers' curriculum thinking beyond the level of just 'subjects', into dimensions related to the teaching and learning needs of children and the contextual demands faced by schools. The books cover areas such as creativity, success and competence, exploration and problem solving, information technology across subjects and boundaries, play in the primary curriculum, questioning and teacher–child interactions, values in relation to equality issues, social, moral and spiritual frameworks, and physical aspects of teaching and learning. Each book has had, within its working title, the rationale of the unique triad of child, teacher and context which underpins all primary schooling and education, for example in this particular case, interaction and communication. This structure serves to emphasize for authors the inextricable and imperative balance in this triad for effective classroom and curriculum practices. The model we have developed and agreed is shown in Figure 1.

All the writers in the series have been concerned to emphasize the quality, nature and extent of existing classroom practices, and how it is possible to build on these sound pedagogical bases. For this reason, chapters within each title often begin with two or more cameos offering features of practice as starting points for teasing out aspects requiring enquiry, analysis, evaluation and discussion. Chapters then develop their own relevant themes but with consistent reference to what these mean to children and teachers within the general autonomy, and constraints, of the school context.

Issues concerning the *child* take their stance from cognitive psychology (as this book does) and include the child as:

- an active searcher after meaning;
- an individual with particular perceptions of the world and their part in it;
- a person who can reflect on their own learning and understanding;
- a learner with his or her own curriculum needs and interests to be considered;
- an interactive person, learning in collaboration with peers and adults;
- a unique individual but also one with collective needs;
- a member of a 'social' community, i.e. home, family, school, wider community.

Aspects to do with the teaching role lay stress on the *teacher* as a reflective and critical professional who will occasionally but regularly need to stand back from day-to-day practice in order to think about and analyse the triadic relationships and to acknowledge:

- their own learning styles and experiences;
- their own beliefs, values, knowledge and conceptual understanding of pedagogy;
- their need to raise questions about practice and find solutions in an ongoing way;
- their role as mutual learners with children and colleagues;
- their responsibilities as facilitators of learning, as models of learning and as negotiators of meaning with children;
- their role in enabling children's learning rather than always in 'teaching';
- their function as observers and assessors of children's understandings as well as outcomes;
- their obligation clearly to conceptualize the whole curriculum of which the National Curriculum is a part.

When we consider the *context* of pedagogy, this focus subsumes such aspects as the learning environment, school ethos and the actual classroom and school. It also includes such elements as:

- the physical environment – indoors and outdoors;
- the social environment of school and schooling (e.g. is the child an outcome of the context or has the context influenced the child?);
- the psychological environment of school and schooling;
- the philosophical considerations within schools and aspects such as teachers' beliefs and values;
- the curriculum context, including the National Curriculum where this is relevant and appropriate, but also showing where this does not necessarily meet pedagogical needs;
- the frameworks within which the whole concept of schooling takes place and where this fits education in a broader sense.

The overall rationale for each book in the series starts from a belief that teachers should be enabled to analyse their own practices in specific aspects of the broader curriculum as a major aspect of their professionalism. The books are particularly useful at a time of continual curriculum change, when reflection is being focused back upon the child and pedagogy generally as the only perpetuating and consistent elements.

As an integral component, all the books weave teachers' assessment of children's learning and understanding into each particular focus, the intention being to show how the planning>learning> assessment>planning cycle is vital to the quality and success of children's and teachers' learning experiences. With their practical ideas, challenges and direct relevance to classroom practice, these books offer ways of establishing theory as *the* adjunct to practice; they build on teachers' thinking about how they already work in the classroom and help teachers to consider how they may enrich, extend and advance their practices to the mutual benefit of themselves, the children, the curriculum and education in society as a whole.

Interactive children, communicative teaching aims to give teachers confidence in approaching the sometimes daunting but always dynamic task of handling information and communication technology (ICT) in terms of their own capabilities and those of the primary children they teach. Deirdre Cook and Helen Finlayson have faced this task with the same flexibility and dynamism they are encouraging in teachers – no mean feat given the ever-changing nature of their focus and the continual, escalating technological changes which are now part of all our lives.

Deirdre and Helen have focused in a clear and matter-of-fact way upon the processes and skills required by computers and some other communicational technologies rather than dwelling on particular software or equipment. They have done this in the belief that, once teachers and children understand the essential nature and substance of ICT in primary education, incessant changes are easier to handle and incorporate into sound, reflective practices. Theories of learning have been closely and neatly related to ICT uses and processes, especially the theory of Vygotsky and the place of supported learning in a sociocultural context. Because we are all in the position of being 'learners' with the new technologies (adults more often than children!) it is important that we all use whatever 'knowledgeable' support is available to us. This book ably serves this purpose in guiding and supporting readers in the principles and practices of using ICT to greatest effect.

Because of its straightforward style, the book will serve to give teachers and other adults in primary classrooms confidence in their own IT capabilities and in the use of ICT with children from nursery through to the end of the primary school. Helen and Deirdre have worked to demystify the often off-putting 'computerspeak' and jargon prevalent in this field and have provided a useful appendix on which readers can draw for current information and advice on appropriate provision of tools and resources for ICT teaching and learning. Another vital feature in these days of home computers is the strong links Deirdre and Helen have emphasized throughout the book on out-of-school and general home uses of ICT which inform and influence children's understanding. The message is that, for good or ill, we have become reliant upon ICT and, in fact, most of us now appreciate the benefits it implicitly provides in our everyday lives. The basis of sound ICT teaching is in being able to work positively with children, utilizing their prior experiences and enabling them to meet a future which will be even more dependent than our present on the new technologies.

The emphasis on the need for, and importance of, play as a means by which to understand and engage with ICT, especially computers, is dear to my heart. Not only is a whole chapter devoted to play ('hard fun' in Helen and Deirdre's words) but the processes of playing to learn and engaging children in this motivational way are interwoven throughout the book, particularly in enabling children to make sense of the kind of symbolism implicit in ICT. This links also with the focus they have given to the notion of 'emergence'; whilst this may be more normally related to literacy and numeracy, it is equally a concept which applies to emerging ICT skills right across the curriculum. For readers who perhaps need to be dragged kicking and screaming into the new technological age presented by such aspects as the world wide web, this is the book to gentle these reactions and offer an emerging boost to confidence and competence.

This short but well conceived book has its greatest strength in that it is not merely written for readers wanting to learn *about* ICT but for those wanting to think about learning and teaching *through* ICT. To get the most out of it, readers will need to interact with the text, which is made easy through the excellent cameos of primary classroom life which serve as a 'scaffold' to teachers' enriched learning. This book provides its own scaffolding, being written by experts in the field who are only too well aware of the practical and conceptual challenges which ICT presents to many primary teachers, but who are committed to supporting children and teachers in capitalizing on the new technologies. So 'interact' with it and allow the book to 'communicate' to you the many joys and benefits of working with ICT in the primary classroom.

Dr Janet Moyles

Acknowledgements

We would like to thank all the children, teachers and colleagues who in any way contributed to the contents of this book by working with us, allowing us to visit their schools or use their photographs of children working with ICT.

Introduction

Today, we live in an *age* of technology. Technology permeates the home, the school, the workplace and even recreation and sport. We find ourselves overtly, as well as unknowingly, reliant upon technological advances in a wide range of ways.

Some of us choose to ignore this technology most of the time, but nevertheless enjoy the possibilities it opens up to us, especially in the area of increased opportunity for leisure pursuits. The home entertainments and information industry has been an area of massive growth. Whole sections of supermarkets are devoted to selling video materials, CDs and music tapes and specialist computer shops proliferate in every high street. These changes, as well as offering possibilities for enjoyment, also offer the prospect of lifelong learning conveniently on tap. Just as the television replaced the hearth as the family focal point (at least in the eyes of the advertisers) the computer manufacturers would now like the world to see their machines as taking over this coveted spot. CD-Roms and web connections increasingly give more convenient and speedy access to information of all kinds. Electronic links make hard-copy encyclopaedias a quaint old-fashioned idea as home computers spread across the land and around the world. Changes in these areas have been rapid and largely welcomed as improving personal choice and facilitating individuals' pursuit of particular interests.

Technological changes are also reflected within education. Children have an entitlement to become competent with technological tools and to use them to enhance their learning across the whole curriculum. This book is about living and learning in this context of technical change and development, and particularly about how this impinges on primary school children and teachers, both experienced classroom practitioners and the new generation of teachers in training.

Teachers and parents will be familiar with theories of learning which emphasize the individual child and the manner in which all children move through a series of stages towards the final destination of mature knowledge. Piaget's work is probably the most famous example of such a perspective. This book, however, looks at learning in a slightly different way, one in which learning in a developmental manner is seen to be embedded in social activities and brought to the learner within a cultural meaning system by other people more skilled and experienced than they are. This viewpoint sees language, especially talk, as of critical importance in the learning process. This is because it is by the use of this 'tool' that learners come to make meaningful judgements about what is going on around them in the everyday practices of home and school.

Children's understandings may at first be imperfect but gradually, as they make sense of more bits of the puzzle, what they 'know' gets closer and closer to that way of knowing which is associated with the way adults 'know' things. The context in which these interactions happen is extremely relevant in terms of what learners are able to learn. Learning in the informal setting of the home and everyday world and the more formal learning associated with schools and classrooms, are not seen as being exactly the same in every respect, but the learning achieved in each of these social situations is very real. Early informal learning offers a firm foundation on which subsequent achievement can rest.

An example of this may be seen in the idea of *emergence*. This is most familiar in early literacy development but increasing interest is given to this idea in the domain of mathematics. Children gradually make sense of the culture in which they live by playing with symbols such as talk, print, numerals, maps and drawing and in their everyday interactions with people more experienced than themselves. Parents and teachers draw their attention to important aspects of these tasks and this helps children to understand how things are done conventionally in the society in which they live. As an illustration of the importance of home experiences in the area on which this book focuses – i.e. information and communication technology (ICT) – it might be helpful to look out for the following elements. *Emergence*, as a process, recognizes children as:

- being actively involved in making sense of things;
- seeking information from others when they need it (peers or adults);
- using what they already know, socially and psychologically;
- requiring the right conditions to demonstrate their understandings;
- gradually mastering the new learning because of their efforts to make sense of the actions they observe and take part in (adapted from Hall 1987).

It is this activity by children which creates the *context* for the learning. *Context*, in the sense we are using it here, is a complex and very important idea. It refers to more than the specific physical time and space in which these learning interactions occur (for more detailed explanations of both Piaget and Vygotsky's views, see Merry 1998.) In this book the idea of context includes:

- the people who are actively engaged with each other to 'do' something;
- the domain in which the interactions occur (home or school or elsewhere);
- the space and time in which these events occur;
- the talk and meaning-making going on between all the people involved;
- societal influences such as gender or ethnicity;
- use of 'tools' such as writing or other artefacts, or in our case computers and other technological devices;
- the computer context, i.e. the learning space created by the hardware and software being used.

Put at its simplest, learning is seen to be firmly located in social activities which are influenced by many things outside the actual time and space in which the learning happens – things which are part of our everyday culture. Over a learning lifetime we gradually become more expert at doing things and then, in turn, help our children to learn the things they need to know to become creatively active and successful in the society in which they will live.

ICT is increasingly a part of that society and will become ever more familiar to children. Its place in school today is not only a reflection of its use in the wider society. ICT has its own contribution to make to education, enhancing the learning process in exciting ways and enabling children to:

- take more control of their own learning;
- access up-to-date information from a wide range of real world sources;
- communicate efficiently with other people on a worldwide scale.

Already in today's classrooms children can question famous present-day artists about their current works or even ask for comment upon the works the class is creating. This has been done through on-line artist-in-residence workshops (Davis 1998). Pupils can even be invited to find out first hand about projects being undertaken by scientists currently involved in research – for example, why making predictions about earthquakes can be so difficult. Many pupils have already taken part in classes being given in different countries and continents through video links, which puts a whole new slant on international communications. Putting their own pictures, stories and poems on a school web page to be read by pupils in linked schools is a wonderful way for children to gain a wider audience for their work and to encourage them to achieve the very highest of presentation standards (Hartland 1998). However, despite all these wonderful possibilities, Ofsted inspections in 1995–6 found that 'only half the primary schools inspected met the requirements of the National Curriculum in IT' (Goldstein 1997: 6).

ICT presents wonderful opportunities as well as challenges for schools endeavouring to find the most satisfactory ways in which every pupil can enjoy the educational experiences which have proved so motivating and beneficial in sponsored projects like those above. As teachers we know that enthusing children about learning and supporting them in gaining new knowledge represents probably the most rewarding aspect of our job. We want to know how best to extend our existing knowledge of pedagogy so that in using ICT effectively we are able to know and practise the positive aspects of the vision of the future which are here already. In this book we are attempting to trace a path to the future, showing how educational ICT can be incorporated into tried and tested primary pedagogy to provide additional opportunities to children without jettisoning sound values and educational ideals.

We start by thinking about education in the home, as many computers are being used there. Chapter 1 reviews various educational activities which technology in the home contributes to children's overall learning. In Chapter 2 we explore the role of play in educational settings as a dynamic approach to learning with ICT. Chapter 3 follows this by considering how ICT and software provide learning tools whose use is guided by the teacher to maximize pupils' learning. Chapter 4 explores learning management and the decisions which need to be made by class teachers in incorporating ICT work in the curriculum. The teacher's role in designing and supporting learning is taken further in Chapter 5, which extends the idea of the social organization of pupils to emphasize the importance of communication. The final chapter develops a perspective on whole school issues which underpin successful ICT development.

Each chapter opens with two or three cameos depicting aspects of classroom life. These may be very similar to incidents which many teachers have seen or actually experienced. From these we try to draw particular points which act as illustrations of some of the actualities of computer use which we hope may be thought-provoking. Most of the chapters are organized in three sections focusing primarily on ICT and the child, the context and the teacher. Chapter 4 is the exception to this, as the context in this particular exploration has been used in a way which emphasizes the learning perspective influencing much of our thinking.

As with all books concerning ICT there are some technical terms to be confronted. We hope that our readers will have patience with us when we have used such terms but we have also provided an appendix with additional explanations and some references to other publications which should be helpful.

As Goldstein points out: 'Many teachers have coped admirably with curricular and technological changes. But much remains to be done to improve professional practice in the teaching of IT, and in its productive use' (Goldstein 1997: 2). Our intention is to encourage teachers and student teachers in training to discuss and debate the role of ICT within education in a way that builds upon their existing knowledge of sound pedagogical principles. From the starting point of exploring the strategic implications of ICT we anticipate that as teachers we will all be better able to achieve that excitement which comes from the successful use of ICT.

1

ICT learning at home and at school

Cameo 1

In a nursery, Jody is using a laptop computer and pressing keys, then examining the screen. 'Oh look – Oscar Orange,' she says as she types in a row of Os. Then 'Kiss, kiss, kiss,' as she types in a row of Xs. Another child, Dale, is looking very busy, using all the fingers of both hands in turn on the keyboard, as an adult typist does. His friend comes to see what he is doing, but Dale waves him away.

'I'm too busy now, I'm too busy doing this to play with you now,' he says.

Cameo 2

Ten-year-old James is a Manchester United fan and has found the address for their web page from the programme of the last match he went to. He does not get to many matches, but can now keep up with the fortunes of the team and his favourite players through the Internet. He is using the family computer in the study at home and opens the web browser. He then types in the web address and gets straight to the Manchester United home page. He skips through some of the advertising at the top and reads the team selection for Saturday's match. Before going any further he adds a bookmark to this page, so that he can get back to it quickly whenever he wants. He then looks up some information about his favourite players, and finds out about the opposing team. He clicks on other highlighted words in the text to find out more about international matches, and learns about the countries as well. He ends up reading about the new sports facilities being built for the next Olympic Games.

Introduction

Every parent as well as every teacher is acutely aware of the importance of developing children's literacy and numeracy capability both for their success in the world of education and of later life. In our increasingly technological age becoming a confident and competent user of ICT is increasingly recognized as vital. Learning about ICT and through ICT are part of both today's and tomorrow's world.

This chapter looks at the role of ICT against the changing background of rapid developments in the information industry and considers the impact this is having on the experience of children and teachers in schools. The government has underlined the importance of the ICT entitlement for both children and teachers (either presently in school or undergoing training) to ensure an 'ICT literate' population in the twenty-first century.

Children currently growing up with our ever-changing technology come to learn about it early. They find out how to set up the video player in much the same way as they learn to use a knife and fork – and at about the same time in their lives. Adults, on the other hand, tend to feel more comfortable with the older, more familiar technology, of which they have achieved mastery. Quite understandably we often feel threatened by the thought of becoming complete novices again when faced with yet another technical innovation.

Many teachers feel much the same way about the rapid expansion of technology into the classrooms where they work, especially when they have not had the opportunity of very much training in using this type of equipment. Some schools have been using both live television broadcasts and video recordings to provide additional material within their teaching for a number of years, and a great deal of good educational material is available from public broadcasts. But these are of a more passive nature than interactive computer use and demand only the ability to set up and switch on the video player. Teachers are, however, special adults with a great deal of expertise and knowledge about children and the way they learn and develop. They have been put in a position, often not of their own choosing, in which they have considerable responsibility for developing children's use and understanding of ICT within the classroom in the context of the overall curriculum. For many teachers all this expansion is happening while they are still developing their own knowledge and skills base in this area of rapid innovatory change. As teachers we recognize that technology offers us an extra dimension to add to our range of teaching strategies and techniques but making meaningful use of these new tools needs to build upon experience of both: remembering successful teaching techniques is as important as acquiring new ICT strategies.

Because technological devices are all around us it is easy to assume that *all* children in our society know a great deal about computers, but this may not be so, as home experience of technology can vary significantly within any group of children. Teachers need to know about pupils' starting points in ICT, as they do in literacy and numeracy, if they are to teach in a way which allows every child to build on existing knowledge and ensures that everyone gets the opportunity to develop further capabilities.

The child

Cameo 1 and Cameo 2 show us children of different ages: a nursery child using a laptop computer in school, and a 10-year-old, using the Internet on the computer at home. Both children show a sophisticated acceptance of the technological age and demonstrate their ability to cope with, and learn through, ICT.

Many parents with children below school age may feel that their children are not ready to cope with adult computers, but discover that the two go very well together; children as young as 3 years can handle computers and interact meaningfully with simple computer programs (Hess and McGarvey 1987; Shade and Watson 1987). Not all software programs available offer instant gratification and users need to make a considerable investment of time to learn to use the program competently. This effort often proves intensely satisfying in the long term for children and adults of all ages. In Cameo 2, the fully networked computer available to James gave him access to a gold mine of information but, as in real mines, the nuggets could be mixed with a great deal of dross. Much of the material available on the Internet is not written with 10-year-old boys in mind. The texts could be too difficult to read or the information too complex to be readily understood, but by introducing a few bookmarked web sites parents could point to the most suitable beginning material. Child users like James could be encouraged to add their own markers whenever they find interesting and accessible network pages.

The children in Cameo 1 are not from especially privileged computer-owning backgrounds but, having seen people like the school secretary using a computer, they know the type of actions to perform. They find the keyboards fascinating and are pleased with their ability to produce letters and other symbols they recognize on the screen. Adults who know the children well are quite surprised at the degree of knowledge about print and text which they exhibit. Opportunities to experiment with writing and its tools are very important parts of the literacy acquisition process and play offers a powerful incentive for learning, a point we will explore more fully in Chapter 2.

Experimenting and learning

The nursery children in Cameo 1 are using open-ended, flexible software on laptop computers. They have a simple word processor which gives large letters on the screen as keys are pressed. The program can also be asked to 'speak' letter sounds or names and read words. Jody identifies the screen displayed letters using the names from a well-known phonics scheme showing that she can relate other learning experiences to this new one. Possibly she gained this knowledge from playing with the computer version of this teaching material (see Wenden, undated). At its simplest this program draws the letter character on the screen when that letter key is pressed. It is used to practise letter-sound recognition. By itself, used by an individual child the program is quite limited, but when it is more imaginatively used within a social context such as the nursery class children can get to know the letter characters and integrate sound and letter knowledge into text-based work. Many such programs provide opportunities for teachers to add-in their own word and letter work and use their own or the children's voices rather than an unknown computer voice. Recently produced software of this kind allows teachers to adjust the sound produced to reflect the complexities of letter-sound correspondences or local variations in speech patterns.

For young children the word processor provides a delightful extension to their other mark-making activities as they discover that holding down a key repeats the letter on the screen. One child watches in fascination as a single letter fills three rows on the screen, then stops as he takes his finger off the key. Older children in the nursery typing in their own names learned to touch the keys lightly to prevent repeated letters. One child recognized her name written by another, but commented that it should begin with 'a big letter'. A 4-year-old using the keyboard then asked the nursery assistant how big letters were made and learned to use the SHIFT key. Yet another child was using the speech facility in the program to listen to different letters and wanted to find 'Ch' to make the beginning sound of his name and wasn't at all satisfied with 'C' and 'H' as pronounced separately by this particular machine.

These children are involved with activities which have important implications for their learning about computers and conventional literacy:

- relating cause and effect to their own activity (e.g. key press and screen change);
- drawing upon knowledge acquired elsewhere (e.g. letter and sound relationships);
- demonstrating understandings drawn from knowledge of signs and their meaning (X as a kiss);
- enacting possible future roles;
- integrating and coordinating various domains of knowledge;
- demonstrating their facility for imitation and showing off their competence;
- making sense in their own way of the social and cultural events of their everyday experiences;
- seeking adult help when their own knowledge proves insufficient to deal with a problem;
- learning about action and reaction (i.e. power sources of 'machines') (adapted from Bruce 1996).

In Cameo 2, James is demonstrating his understanding, drawing on knowledge acquired from elsewhere and meeting several other aspects of learning listed above. His basic understanding of navigation in the Internet enables him to find specific information for which he is searching and allows him to relate his new-found football knowledge to his existing store of information. The children in the cameos are all working with powerful adult equipment, not toys. In both cameos the children clearly have specific purposes in mind in their activities even though these may not always match the teacher's or parent's purpose in putting them in that situation. Learning with ICT has both intended and unanticipated gains for both learners and teachers.

Children's attitudes towards computers

The presence of technological equipment in the home – whether for family entertainment, parental work activities or whatever – is increasingly the reality of everyday living for many children, although sadly there will always be some children who don't enjoy these advantages. Nevertheless almost all children will be aware of computers in daily life; they will have seen hole-in-the-wall cash machines and supermarket checkouts as well as games machines and toys, if only in shops, catalogues or through that most powerful and seductive channel of communication, television advertisements. In schools and nursery classes they will certainly come across computers. While for some from the most technologically well-endowed homes these might even be rather old-fashioned machines, almost everyone approaches them with happy anticipation of their chance to 'have a go'.

Children rarely seem to fear computers and when offered the opportunity readily want to copy the actions of adult users. Those with home computer experience may be held to start school with some distinct advantages. From their home experiences children may know how to use the machine; they may also have been helped to use their own children's programs on the computer and be capable of independent computer play. Children naturally want to use machines of all kinds because there is a 'grown-upness' which carries with it associated, positive images, and this is especially true for new technology.

Those who have not met computers before entry to more formal educational settings may need some help and supportive encouragement in getting started so that they too may become able to play readily with the computer and investigate what it does. Children, like our nursery players, are happily unaware of the expense or complexity of many computers. They do not share adult concerns about wasting time or losing hard-learned skills with pens and pencils, or conceptual knowledge relating to spelling or computation. Neither are they concerned with losing the results of their efforts through some caprice of the machine or some negligent actions, something which most adults have experienced if the horror stories they exchange can be given credence! Children's confident approach to exploration provides a vital foundation for ICT learning and should be fostered and encouraged: it is upon this base that teachers are able to begin building bridges to learning of a more specifically curriculum-orientated type.

Learning in a social context

As the cameos illustrate, children are able to bring an awareness of the social world into their learning. Current views about children's learning give much greater attention to the social and cultural dimensions of the situations in which learning takes place than was formerly the case (Vygotsky 1978). The ways in which children bridge the gap between what they learn in one situation and how they can apply it in another are increasingly becoming discussed in research (Ferrera *et al.* 1986; Wood 1988; Engestrom 1996). Cameo 1 shows us something about social context as well as about the less-than-perfect knowledge children have acquired so far. Dale has acquired the physical gestures of the process and is incorporating these in an approximation of the adult's actions but has probably not understood very much else as yet.

It is not a new idea that children in their learning choose to watch and imitate the behaviour of others, usually people the children think of as socially desirable models (Case 1985). James would have learned to use the Internet by watching his parents or older siblings use it and picked up his interest in football from a similar source. Parents might not always approve of every choice of model adopted by their children but they will certainly be aware of the influences of this type of learning. Vygotsky and those who find his view of learning to be helpful feel that the origins of children's learning are to be found in their social interactions with adults and peers who are more experienced with something new than they are themselves. While these people help young learners in a number of ways, learners themselves are very active in this process of 'appropriating' to themselves the knowledge they need to operate successfully in the culture in which they find themselves. All the children in the cameos were doing this: taking and making their own aspects of such adult behaviours.

The context

Learning in the everyday world mostly occurs when individuals come into contact with others or their ideas either directly in face-to-face interactions or indirectly through books or other visual forms of communication. Learning has a 'social' dimension, it occurs initially between people. The social context in which the nursery children were playing with the laptops supported their learning because they could talk to interested adults and friends about what they were doing, make suggestions to each other to extend their knowledge or request relevant help appropriately. This is also true when they are playing and learning with people and toys at home. Having friends or parents around them when they play provides children with a context in which they can talk about what is happening to them and describe what they are doing and why. This type of talk allows children and adults to clarify any misunderstandings jointly to exploit the game's potential. Even James, looking up his football heroes by himself, is motivated by social considerations. He will probably share his knowledge with his friends. If they can't get together immediately they can compare notes in friendly rivalry when they next meet. If James's friends work with him on the Internet, then a session will be likely to last twice as long and the information they access will be better remembered because of their discussion.

The electronic context of home and school

Children are bombarded even in their homes by advertising designed to encourage them to want 'highly desirable' electronic toys and games. If they have no such toys or games at home, then their friends from school may well have, and there is an enormous variety of such resources in the shops. Even if children are not surrounded by electronic gadgets at home or living in homes linked to the Internet they will undoubtedly be aware of many technological devices and playthings. Many toys and games will claim to be educational and several kinds will be found in schools. Examples of these include:

- button-operated talking toys;
- story-ware, talking picture or story books;
- 'mock computers' with sets of different tasks;

- games consoles for older children;
- remote or button-controlled robots;
- simple electronic calculators;
- graphical calculators;
- electronic diary organizers;
- palmtop computers;
- laptop computers;
- personal home computers;
- fully networked home office systems.

Children can develop their electronic sophistication from any of these with which they come into contact, particularly if they see an adult or older child making use of them. But some electronic gadgets have more educational potential than others. The reason for this is the open-endedness, or flexibility, of their use. In schools, calculators, reading toys and robots may make their appearance for this very reason.

Reading support toys

Here we mean story boards or reading games where stories can be read by the machine and animations or sounds produced by touching the screen with a lightpen or clicking the mouse. Potentially, reading support toys have a great deal to offer in encouraging children to read. Early research on computer-based talking books suggests that enjoyment and motivation may be the biggest gains (Scoresby 1996; Miller *et al.* 1997). While no one would deny that these are hugely important aspects of learning to read there are some other important factors to bear in mind too (see Underwood and Underwood 1997). When children use these talking stories they tend to spend time looking at the animations, which can prove a distraction from the story-line. However, the very powerful combination created by linking spoken text with the words printed on the page, which is constantly available, offers considerable support for inexperienced readers: a link which has so far not been fully explored.

Robots

Other electronic toys available in large toy shops, such as robots, do not look at all like computers or involve the use of a display screen. They may, however, provide a very good introduction to

Figure 1.1 Intense concentration as children key commands into floor turtle 'Roamer'

computers. These battery-operated programmable toys often take the form of a science-fiction robot or vehicle. Common examples in schools are 'Roamer', a round grey dome with eyes pointing forwards (see Figure 1.1), and Pip, a square black box, but there are others sold mainly to the home market. What all these toys have in common is that they can be given a sequence of commands for actions to be carried out involving movements and changes of direction. Commands are entered through a control panel which may be an integral part of the robot, or a separate infrared or radio-linked control pad. Such toys can be regarded as 'computer devices', because they are programmable, and they provide considerable open-ended possibilities for children's experimentation. Two important points about programmable robots make them educationally valuable:

1 A sequence of commands can be used, rather than a single action on a single button.

2 They require numerical input – for example, to say how far and in what direction the robot should go in each move.

In the home many devices are spoken of as being 'computer controlled' or 'programmable': washing machines or compact-disc players, for example. These have electronic components which enable particular actions to be selected in advance, but only in relation to the specific job for which they have been designed – i.e. washing clothes or playing music. These are outside our main consideration of ICT, although children gain a great deal of information and confidence from watching and helping adults use these devices. Increasingly central in domestic settings are very flexible personal computers which run a wide range of software. Many other devices carry out a useful but more limited range of tasks: word processors or calculators for example. Figure 1.2 illustrates one way of visualising this range of electronic applications.

All the electronic devices featured in Figure 1.2 are characterized by having three main components:

1 An input device.
2 A central processor.
3 An output device.

This makes them responsive to and controllable by the users, so they are *interactive*. In the centre of the 'flower' is the personal computer – the most flexible tool for a wide range of learning activities. Surrounding this are a range of computerized tools and toys which have full interactive facilities, responding in different ways to different inputs, but which are limited in the range of activities they encompass. Moving outwards we find a range of similar-seeming gadgets but these have a much more limited range of actions, lacking in both flexibility and interactivity. At the far edges of the flower are electronic devices for specific actions only, but all contain some internal programs which can be selected by the user.

Children's experience with any of these items, more particularly those nearest the centre of the flower can give them a very confident start to their formal ICT education. This education may well involve the use of some 'home appliances', particularly simple word processors, calculators and robots, and we have these applications in mind when we talk of 'computers' throughout this book.

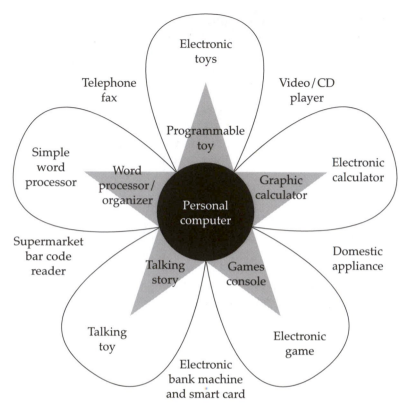

Figure 1.2   Electronic applications

The teacher

We have offered a picture of enthusiastic and confident young experimenters eager to find out more about the grown-up world, looking for opportunities and information which will help them. How then do we teachers feel? Some of us are, no doubt, just as confident and eager as the children in our scenarios but others may have more mixed feelings. The discussion of the cameos has indicated that playful exploration of new experiences is an important dimension of learning but adults, whether parents or teachers in school, may not feel they have freedom to play with these new toys in the uninhibited way shown by the children. Adults are only too aware of the complexity and expense of these machines. They may have also experienced difficulties in getting programs to load properly, or in saving work. But at the same time teachers readily recognize that a high status activity such as computer play, in which children want to involve themselves, has many positive advantages in motivating pupils to engage with the learning process in the classroom. So, teachers too need time to 'play about' with new technology to identify the learning potential which it offers and devise ways of harnessing technological power to enhance and extend existing teaching strategies.

Evidence of early learning

The children in Cameo 1 were 'playing' with computers within an imaginative setting in much the same way as they would with any other nursery play materials. Doing so gave them the opportunity to display their existing knowledge and in this way provided a rich source of information for their teachers. Teachers looking for evidence of learning find that careful observations enable them to identify attainment, plan subsequent activities and develop appropriate ways in which to present these so that an active and challenging programme can be planned which allows the learning needs of individual children to be met within the overall curriculum framework (see Chapter 2 for detailed suggestions).

Observations were used by nursery staff in our first cameo to identify children's understanding of literacy as well as their familiarity with computer keyboards, and the children showed that they could cope with some sophisticated ideas. Such informal observations could be developed into other formats such as checklists or record sheets which could form part of the teacher's overall assessment procedures. By identifying for themselves what they consider to be key aspects of learning for their pupils in the area of ICT, teachers could then use these assessment instruments to check for progress and development over a period of weeks or months. In our scenario the children's playful behaviours led the staff to outline the following list of things to look out for:

- Does the child look expectantly at the screen when a key is pressed?
- Does the child deliberately change the pressure and time of key presses to give single letters, or strings of repeated letters at will?
- Does the child discriminate or notice any difference between letters, numbers or punctuation marks?

- Does the child look for specific letters or match the upper case keyboard letters with the lower case screen presentation?
- Does the child use the SHIFT, SPACE, DELETE or RETURN keys?
- Does the child comment on what is happening?
- Does the child ask adults or peers for information, advice or help when working?

Looking for signs of progression

Teachers need to be able to establish for themselves a view of the *ICT starting point* of each of the children within their class. When children enter school for the first time, either to nursery or reception classes some of the necessary information will come from the teacher's own observations, but parents can be consulted about the kinds of technological devices and computer activities familiar to their children. The children too can have their say: every bit of information is useful for building up a picture of achievement.

Starting with a complete new class is, however, rather different, since admissions policies for starting school vary from area to area and this creates a whole range of different patterns. Some teachers need to get to know a large number of children very quickly, whereas others will meet a few at a time at intervals throughout the year. With a new class or large group teachers need to find out what the children know, understand and can do with respect to computers as quickly as possible. Cohorts moving up within one educational setting will have ICT records (considered in Chapter 6). Even with these to hand most teachers will want to establish firmly their own expectations about appropriate behaviour as well as outlining the standards towards which they expect children to aim. In addition to making the kinds of observations already mentioned, teachers may find it useful to have a checklist of the key things they feel it is important for pupils to know. Such a checklist may ask if every child is:

- fully informed about safety;
- able to switch on and load specific programs;
- able to save and print at appropriate points;
- capable of working with a partner.

Most schools will have general guidelines about such matters but individual teachers may want to be more specific about the level of responsibility they expect children to take for their own computer work. Guidelines may need to be established about such things as storing and caring for disks, batteries and printers. It seems reasonable, for example, to expect children from the reception class onwards to be able to switch the computer on when it has been safely plugged in by an adult. Similarly, loading a program should be readily manageable by the majority of children. They won't learn to do this instantly, so they need to be given plenty of time and help in the early stages of familiarization with the program to enable them to reach the required degree of independence.

Establishing continuity of learning

Research in Australia found that neither at home nor at school do children get a lot of help once they have learned how to get into a program (Downes 1996). This is an important issue when we consider continuity and progression in children's learning experiences. Teachers may also find that even experienced home computer users have some 'bad habits' which they want to discourage – things such as switching the machine off before the program has been closed, or printing work before it has been saved, both of which can cause problems for the next user and make the classroom management of ICT tasks that much more demanding on the class teacher.

When considering starting points for first computer activities with a new class, whatever their age and whatever the curriculum context of the lesson (e.g. art, using a paint package to investigate using light and shade within colours, or history, investigating a database containing the census materials from a local area 100 years ago) it might be worth thinking about some of the following strategies:

- Doing a large group or class demonstration, asking the children at each stage to tell you what you should do next, and why. This will allow you to reinforce safety rules as well as quickly show you gaps in the children's knowledge.
- Using volunteers to demonstrate mouse skills and computer knowledge when it comes to printing out or saving work with a particular piece of software. This could be followed by an activity in which pairs of pupils take turns in using the same

software. This will help identify children who are going to need further support.

- Inviting children to bring into school their power toys (battery, mains or clockwork operated), which they can then demonstrate, explaining how they work and how they have to be looked after. This could be used to introduce notions of power and energy to put computers into context, and to extend discussions on safety and care of equipment.

- Creating weekly computer child monitors, to be the 'experts' for particular programs being used that week – for instance, the history database investigation. It might be useful to have a little team of two or three pupils who would act as consultants to the other children on particular aspects of the database work. During the week when the class are interrogating the database, the team can have some extra training in helping others to make sure that their questions match the way the data is presented in the data file. They would also be able to help novices remember the sequence of steps to start a new search. This means systematically working through the class so that every child has some opportunity to carry out this role in an appropriately demanding way.

The last idea in the list may require advance planning. Most classes we have been into have one or two 'computer bright sparks' who are called upon to sort out minor problems. It is certainly useful to be able to use class expertise in this way, but it needs careful handling not only because it can be very unfair to the children who are overused, but also because it is unfair to the children who never seem to get called upon in this way. It is very easy to see that they may feel they are overlooked and under-valued. As teachers, we need to ensure that everyone gets to be a 'computer expert' in some way at some times. Everyone needs to extend their own range of expertise. Emergent experts, whatever their skill level, all need some personal training to help them take on the role. The outcome of investment of teacher time here will not only lead to increased pupil confidence but will encourage the cascading of existing knowledge throughout the class.

Recording assessment evidence

The process of discovering children's existing knowledge of computer use and of setting standards for them to achieve in taking responsibility here will, of necessity, involve the teacher in collecting information worth keeping. Teachers and pupils will be involved in producing written information which will provide useful evidence at a later date. Much of this writing will be done quite informally initially, for example, the notes teachers make during activities such as those suggested for meeting a new class or comments made when they make notes about what each child has achieved, or any difficulties they might have. Children themselves can list any electronic toys or describe any home computer experiences: all such notes might usefully be kept. Creating child monitors will need to be done systematically and this will be recorded. Such plans should include:

- information about the time set aside for training;
- the order in which children get individual opportunities;
- the area in which their existing expertise is to be further developed;
- evaluations of how effectively monitors carried out their tasks.

In introducing children to new programs it is of course essential to ensure that all pupils have appropriate opportunities to achieve ICT learning goals. Written records are most important here. Children need to develop competence and confidence in their own abilities to adapt to technological changes as they arise.

Summary

This chapter has considered the place of technology in everyday life and the rapid rate of change associated with its usage. Links between home and school learning with technology have been explored to consider what we need to know about pupils' prior knowledge and experiences in order to plan appropriately for their future learning in school. The centrality of what is to be learnt and the question of how best to achieve the results we, as teachers, want have been identified as of great importance.

Points to consider

The following activities are suggestions for INSET work within school to consider issues which may be relevant to your particular situation.

1 Choices have to be made by parents and teachers about which technological devices and software programs they feel are appropriate for children in their care to use. These choices cannot be made in a vacuum. Features such as the acceptability to parents, children or teachers, age appropriateness of hardware and software, learning purposes and social dimensions such as home or school use are all important. Outline ways in which parents and teachers can cooperate to build an overall picture of an individual child's technological world.

2 Produce a schedule as part of an overall baseline assessment pack to cover ICT knowledge and skills at school entry.

3 Not everyone is thrilled by children's increasing involvement with ICT. Parents and teachers worry that this process might lead to increasing pupil isolation or be seen as a substitute for good quality teaching. If computer use is not an end in itself, list the important safeguards you would want to see in place in either home or school settings to ensure that neither of the two outcomes listed above are likely to come about.

2

Taking play seriously

Cameo 1

In a small rural school the 'middle' mixed Year 3/4 class has spent this half of the term investigating 'Space World', a computer adventure game in which each group of children plays the role of the crew of a spaceship which has landed on a new planet. Their various curriculum activities connected to this adventure have involved life on earth as well as life in space – for example, planning real investigations into how things grow on earth and the variety of creatures to be found in various habitats. The space focus has provided many opportunities for the children to use their imaginations to the full by paralleling in the space dimension the idea of habitats and related life forms, which has allowed them to invent monsters, plants and small furry inhabitants for their new world. In both dimensions the children have had to grapple with many problems while thinking about themselves, their team members and fellow players. Pupils have been working in small similar ability groups, each group engaged in one of several activities related to Space World which span many dimensions such as aesthetic and creative, scientific and technological, linguistic, moral, social and personal learning. Looking around the classroom we can see three children following screen directions using a map they are building up of the imaginary planet, and another group using boxes, batteries, wires and assorted bits to build a robotic guard. Others seem to be developing a piece of impromptu drama. The teacher is talking to a group who are searching through information book indices checking out bog-loving plant species.

Cameo 2

It is Saturday afternoon at a well-known electrical chain store where a wide range of devices are displayed and customers are invited to try them out for themselves. A boy and his father are playing with a tiny electronic organizer. The father is pressing keys to see if he can find out where the word-processing facility is, while the son is showing his father how the organizer links to the Internet. If it's easy, he thinks, his dad might buy it, and then . . . wow . . . cool!

Cameo 3

Five and 6-year-old children are busy in their classroom, involved in a range of activities. One group of four are playing in their travel agent's shop. Two, Sara and Davina, are customers choosing a holiday from a selection of brochures while the others work behind the counter. One of the latter, Heather, has a small notepad computer and the other, Nell, a small word processor. Both are engrossed in their role. Heather is carefully typing in her customer's name, address and destination, paying careful attention to spelling and typing accurately with some help from her customer. Nell is more flamboyantly and rapidly pressing the keys, happily creating a text with which both she and her customer are content and which both know contains all the important information even if this lacks what others might feel to be important conventional details (see Figure 2.1).

Introduction

The cameos contain examples of adults and children of different ages playing which vary in terms of setting (e.g. classroom, imaginative-play corner, shop) and computer context (e.g. technology involved, program content, group composition, sharing of various kinds of expertise, turn taking).

All the cameos contain examples of real and important opportunities for the players to learn a considerable number of different things. Before taking a more detailed look at some of these learning opportunities consideration needs to be given to how play and learning are related to one another. The term 'play' covers a vast range of activities which bring to mind all kinds of feelings, thoughts and opinions, some – but not all – with very positive associations.

Figure 2.1   The travel agent play scenario

This chapter considers the relationship between play, learning, computer knowledge and skills. Play as a means of investigation is particularly pertinent to using computer programs for the first time. Both adults and children make sense of new programs and computers by playing with them to find out what they do, how they do it and what uses the operator can make of them (Moyles 1989).

Play is not always to be thought of as a frivolous or light-hearted activity for although it can undoubtedly contain these elements within itself, play has a very real and serious functional role in learning processes. Langer (1997) discusses how in our everyday life a play activity can become serious work and equally how a person's work activity is often another's favourite recreational pastime. An activity like solving a mathematical problem would be many people's idea of hard work, yet others spend time and money on puzzle books full of such things. It is not the activities themselves which make them into play or work but other aspects of the situation which influence the way we feel about being involved in them.

Play in different contexts can have different functions and purposes. It seems reasonable to assume that play in educational settings should have clear objectives relating to learning (Moyles 1989). The model of learning which informs this book has play as a very central and critical activity. It sees play as being 'a *leading activity*' (Vygotsky 1978: 103) in developing the intellectual ability of the child. Play, as the term is used in this socio-cultural model, requires two essential components:

1 The presence of an imaginary situation.
2 The rules implicit in this situation.

The rules of play are very important: children can only enter into play if they voluntarily accept these rules and abide by them. The rules gain their strength from the children's enjoyment of the game and the commitment to it which all players must share if it is to continue. In one sense play is always a learning activity because children playing must grasp what the rules are and understand how these operate as a system within their play activities. There can be many levels of sophistication in play and its rules, as each of the cameos in some way demonstrates.

Play when looked at in this way, especially when it involves ICT, becomes largely a matter of representation or symbolic activity, emphasizing meaning-making from its very earliest beginnings. It is about becoming a fully functioning member of the social group and society to which you belong, being able to use and understand its tools, signs and artefacts – such things as spoken and written language, numerical and other mathematical symbol systems, maps, diagrams, pictures and music. Children as they grow and develop need to increase their competence in these areas. Two things help. First, it is in play that they become able to separate out some of the strands of symbolic representation which will help them become capable of abstract thinking and able to take control over their own actions and decision making. Second, it is in play of this kind that learning opportunities are created for more experienced people, whether children or adults, to assist in improving the performance of the novice through joint involvement episodes (Schaffer 1996). This activity space is sometimes called the 'zone of proximal development' (ZPD), and is important because we need to see not only what a child can do alone but also explore what can be achieved potentially by that child with some help. The ZPD encompasses present knowledge and future learning potential as well as the importance of the teacher (Vygotsky 1978 and many other subsequent texts – see, for example, Daniels 1996; Merry 1998).

The child

One way of describing Cameo 1 might be to suggest that some children are giving serious attention to the problem – that is, working – while others just 'playing about'. But play is never the obverse of work and all the children's activity in this classroom is purposeful, directed towards the achievement of specific goals. These children are aware of the imaginative dimension of the computer world and of their allotted roles in the space crew. In carrying out their various activities they are able to speak and act both as themselves and as the person they have become in the adventure game. Their actions are constrained by the conditions of the imaginary dimension – danger lurks around the space vehicle and the unknown threatens the unwary every second. They bring to this situation all their real-world knowledge and practical problem-solving abilities to engage with the adventure in a fully committed manner and become involved in:

- problem analysis;
- strategic thinking;
- logical reasoning;
- negotiated decision making;
- recall and reorganization of existing information;
- analysis of team strengths and available resources;
- evaluation of possible problem solutions.

(The second and third items in the list are cognitive skills: see Nicolopoulou and Cole (1993) for an in-depth analysis of this blend of games play and learning.)

In 'Space World' play and imagination have been integrated into a system and built into an item of software designed to meet educational objectives. They work together in a way which creates a dynamic approach to learning. Additionally, the rules of both the classroom setting and the imaginary world have a major and very important part in creating a culture of truly effective collaborative learning. Play is a prototype of those activities which dominate the adult world and which only become possible when personal self-discipline and self-determination are part of the voluntary shared acceptance of the rules of any situation, such as might be found in the world of business or other real-world contexts.

The information presented to the children through electronic communication motivates them to engage with the various challenging tasks within the adventure sequence. They need to help each other to progress through the program's increasingly demanding levels of complexity and this requires them to:

- readily ask for and offer help;
- share their existing knowledge of the curriculum areas which have been touched upon and of the wider world;
- explain their own specific solutions;
- experience both the expert and novice roles;
- acknowledge being wrong;
- remember or keep records of strategies and outcomes;
- read literally and intertextually the problems presented through the various modes;
- develop a joint sense of commitment to achieving a successful outcome;
- collaborate and cooperate socially and intellectually;
- develop effective ICT communication skills such as using a variety of electronic representational systems.

Cameo 2 shows different elements of play, where players create their own imaginary situation of 'if I owned this what could I get it to do for me?' Each has a specific goal in mind and their playful exploration of this cultural object is governed by the rules of that goal. We might surmise that the father would feel justified in playing if this led to more effective work practices in the longer term. This end can only be achieved by his exploring and playing with the computer device and its applications, while the son perhaps occupies the role of the more experienced other, knowing intuitively that further constructive play opportunities for himself rely on the 'user-friendly' characteristics of this new toy. The exploratory play of the son is opening up a whole new world of potential learning for the father. In their play both are working towards mastery of a very important cultural tool and gaining basic knowledge and skill in so doing.

Cameo 3 focuses rather more closely on the use of the computer within play itself. The two critical characteristics of play are present in all the cameos, but the level of sophistication and the goals of the play are different. Whether these are set by the players or by some other means is not as significant in this view of play and learning as in others because of the interrelationship existing between novice and expert within the ZPD they have created and the task which they share.

> Play creates a zone of proximal development in the child. In play the child always behaves beyond his average age, above his daily behaviour; in play it is as though he were a head taller than himself. As in the focus of a magnifying glass, play contains all developmental tendencies in a condensed form and is itself a major source of development.
>
> (Vygotsky 1978: 20)

Risk taking, which is itself an important element of learning, when it happens within a supportive structure such as the ZPD, is not threatening because the learner knows that help is readily available when it is needed.

The young children in Cameo 3 are operating in an imaginary world governed by the rules of society which exist in that world. The level of understanding which our young customers and travel agents have of this is variable and it may be imperfect in our adult eyes, but it allows the children to experiment with the meaning of words and signs within social settings. Each pair of children is at a different stage in this process although they are obviously experienced players who can sustain the complex ideas and relationships which are required when you play at being someone else.

The Vygotskian view of play and learning is powerful because it always takes into account the impact of the social and psychological dimensions on learners and their learning activity. It thinks of learning as going 'beyond the skin', of it being created *between* people and not only within an individual. The list of essential conditions put forward by Cambourne (1986) in relation to development of talk (the first symbol system mastered by children) is extremely helpful in looking at their mastery of tools, signs and artefacts in reading, writing and mathematics especially within the type of symbolic play outlined in the cameos. The conditions required are shown in Figure 2.2.

In Cameo 3 it is easy to see that Sara, Davina, Heather and Nell have had experience of the situation they are playing. They have clearly been present in a shop while real customers and their advisers were demonstrating how negotiations are accomplished.

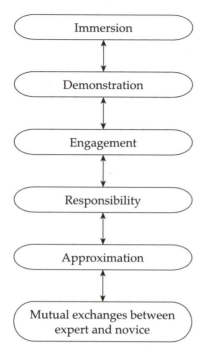

Figure 2.2 Cambourne's list of essential conditions relating to the development of talk
Source: Cambourne (1986: 9).

The children are engaged in their exploration of this activity, making sense of what they have observed and are acting towards each other in a responsible and cooperative effort to establish for themselves the full meaning of this familiar situation. Evidence that immersion and demonstration have and are occurring is offered. Responsibility, too, lies with the children although they may seek adult help (information) when they want it.

Their actions indicate that they have incorporated different levels of approximation successfully into their understanding. Heather is using the computer to demonstrate evidence of her understanding of symbolic representations of various kinds (letters, symbols and the conventions associated with reading and writing). She indicates conventional and adult-like conceptions of literacy. Nell is enacting a less developed approximation of the world as she sees it. The actions and emotions she remembers are much more significant for her than textual accuracy.

The use of computers in play offers children the opportunity to make sense, and come to a mature understanding of, what computers do and how to make them do it, *if* they are allowed experiences like those outlined above. In play children are building meanings among themselves and approximations are acceptable. Symbolic play can be seen as a series of sense-making activities which involve trying out ideas as well as 'trying on adult roles for size'!

Feeling secure in their play environment will mean that even unadventurous children can be encouraged to play with the computer and perhaps gently be nudged towards developing confidence and increasing their overall ICT skill development. The value of this type of play to young children lies in their:

- confident handling of equipment;
- repeated practise of important manipulative skills;
- using language to construct a dialogue between themselves and within themselves;
- engaging in discussion in order to compare understandings or interpretations;
- jointly solving problems;
- organizing the learning effort and seeking help when needed from peers and teachers;
- taking increasing responsibility for the task as their skill increases;
- resolving differences of opinion as they arise in their joint activity;
- integrating their social and psychological knowledge gradually to make sense of their world;
- developing their awareness of the purposes for which word-processing packages can be used;
- extending their understanding of the use of technology in the workplace.

The place of talk in play, the learning processes themselves and the playful exploration of experiences are all important, but so too is the role of adults.

Adult roles in play and learning

In a very detailed study of kindergarten pupils and their computer play with symbols Labbo (1996) describes the idea of 'screenland' to outline how children use the computer to build up understandings between themselves about the different types of symbols they are able to make and use on the screen. The 18 study children had free access to two computers and usually stayed playing in the activity area for about 20 minutes at a time. The children were encouraged to talk about what they were doing and thinking when they created their screens and printouts of symbols. They played with software which had write and draw features and were able to create different effects. The children worked at finding meanings for their created symbols within the multiple representational systems of talk, text and illustration. Playing with the screen images, they created in the same ways as other researchers have found children create in the early stages of writing, drawing and mathematics – i.e. they strove to represent their ideas and to communicate them to other people (Ferreiro and Teberosky 1983; Sinclair 1983; Cook 1998).

Labbo concludes by listing the many benefits the children gained from their play, commenting for example on 'the delight and pleasure in their aesthetic creations', and noting the children's attainments in terms of 'the social and personal empowerment through the elevated status they achieved when they became proficient with particular software and effects' (1996: 381). Multiple literacies such as those described by Labbo are increasingly important for learning. They are not an essentially different type of literacy learning to that with which we are already familiar but the tools and processes represent the synthesis between new technologies and new forms of representation. Time to play, talk, explore and think about activities is a vital aspect of children's learning and should be encouraged and approved of by all adults in as positive a manner as that shown by the adults who helped the children in the study kindergarten. Our knowledge of the ways in which we think about multiple literacies as well as the impact of technology on existing and new literacies continues to grow in importance (see Kress 1997; Lankshear 1997).

Adult involvement in imaginative play is often a source of debate but in the sociocultural model being put forward here adults have much to offer children in the development and extension of their play. In Cameo 1 the adult, in this case the class teacher, has already made a significant 'behind the scenes' contribution to what is happening. The teacher here has acted as 'author or scene setter' for the overall learning experience by designing a cross-curricular range of activities, both on and off the computer, which allow the imaginary dimension of the play to be exploited fully. The rules of that imaginary setting and those of the classroom need to be skilfully blended so that the teacher's planned learning objectives can be realized. In order to achieve this the teacher may need to act as a co-player, director or expert adviser at various times, especially if the children find themselves unable to deal with a specific problem or situation. Then they may need to know where and how to find scientific information, for example, or how to resolve the personal conflicts which may occur within their team activities.

Cameo 2 is more about adults and children sharing and changing roles insofar as each is contributing something different to the situation. The father brings a great deal of world knowledge to bear on his decision making and is, perhaps, less aware than the son of the technical functions the organizer offers. Both are playing in an exploratory manner to check out and share their individual perceptions of the machine's potential. The father will make the final decision but the child may be able to offer some expert advice. The cameo therefore demonstrates something rather closer to a play partnership.

In Cameo 3 the adult role is very similar to that outlined in Cameo 1 in terms of the advance preparation and decision-making processes about learning, appropriate activities and resourcing, but the play itself is very much more within the children's power to direct. The classroom organization defines acceptable behaviours and the setting and resources 'coerce' the role play by activating the social rules within the everyday world. The teacher here will have a much greater involvement as a co-player, as a source of knowledge about tests and literate actions as well as a technological adviser about how the hardware or software works. The children in this cameo are learning *about* ICT rather more than those in Cameo 1. At the same time they are learning *through* ICT about the orthographic conventions of English and about the relationships between the sound of the language and its written representation. The older pupils in Cameo 1, having had such early experiences, are using ICT to help *with* their learning in a range of subject areas, and interpersonally. The adult role changes accordingly, bearing in mind that learning and play are about both present and future potential. Adult involvement is essential to ensure that this progression occurs, and requires teachers to actively monitor and assess the quality of computer play in order to intervene effectively.

The context

Socio-cultural learning theory has always given considerable attention to the contexts in which children grow and develop and the ways these impact on learning. The contexts described so far have been both an actual space as well as a classroom climate and linguistic framework. Equally important is the recognition that children have a valuable contribution to make in defining the play context. This does not mean that children have to build and resource their activities but rather that they should understand how the activity space can be used, what house rules apply to those playing there, and how they can develop and extend the area (with teacher agreement if it is a major innovation they have in mind!). Play contexts should not be the outcomes simply of adult decisions on space, time, resourcing and the potential learning focus. Play is not a process which can be conveniently broken down into bite-sized chunks to be made available at ten-minute intervals. Purposeful contexts for ICT play require:

- the availability of a range of devices – videos, e-mail, full-sized computers, notepads, laptops, fax machines, intercom links or whatever else an inventive teacher can beg, borrow or otherwise get their hands on;
- a range of educational and games-type software;
- links to be made to other learning activities;
- opportunities to engage in activities and processes which reflect the social patterns of everyday life;
- time to play around with each and every form of representational symbol system which will be encountered in other aspects of the school curriculum – e.g. talk, written language, number symbol systems, music, drawing, map-making and diagrammatic work using IT support;
- a recognition by the teacher of what is really happening in the play context;
- planned interactions and involvement in play by the teacher;
- teacher monitoring of children's progress in this form of learning.

Over time, and with increasing levels of confidence, control and cognitive sophistication, pupils should be enabled to move from a position in which their play relates predominately to the question 'What will this do?' through 'How does it work?' to 'What can I really make it do for me?' (see Moyles 1989).

Linguistic context

The chief driving force in this learning through play process will be the discourse (talk) which surrounds the various activities taking place. Playing with words *is* important. Evidence suggests that it can be through playfulness in their own language use that teachers entice children into engagement with them in discussion and other conversational exchanges (Cook 1998). It is the moves in conversation that allow meaning-making to happen between individuals. But true conversation in classrooms is difficult to establish because of the teacher's superior knowledge and level of power, as well as the organizational constraints of classroom life. Play, however, provides children and adults with a more equitable basis for using language and other sign systems such as writing, number or musical notations to make sense of what is happening around them. It allows everyone to discuss aspects of interest on mutual terms. In play with computers, teachers and peers can comment on what they each see as key features of the situation. They can use the existing knowledge they share to solve problems. Sometimes the teacher or more experienced player can use enhanced knowledge to structure the learning of the other by using hints, suggestions and advice which challenges the novice to respond in a more sophisticated manner than might be achievable without the prompts. In the verbal exchanges associated with the types of play outlined in each of our cameos children learn to accept and deal with challenges, to offer explanations, to amend their views in accordance with the opinions of others and to predict how things might turn out.

If we add to Cameo 3 the information that these children are also developing as bilingual speakers then we could speculate that, confident in their play, they have arrived at an explicit agreement about the organization of the joint activity and they know who is doing what. In their selected roles they can use their word processing to:

- write for their own self-determined purpose;
- take risks without fearing 'failure' or negative evaluations of their early efforts;
- gain practice in associating the sounds and corresponding letter symbols of English;
- obtain reinforcement and feedback from the machine about their developing understandings of this relationship by using the speech facility;

- begin to make judgements about word order in English as they listen to the speech facility;
- control the level of repetition they require;
- listen to each other, and modify their response in the light of others' comments;
- use both mother tongue and English in their discussion;
- experience joy in their learning and sharing, both so important and so valuable.

Making decisions about quality in playful learning is neither a straightforward nor a simple task. Each of us comes to the judgement-making required here with a great deal of personal baggage. Our beliefs about the ways in which children learn, our personal philosophies of education, the constraints which affect our ability to carry out classroom engagements as we would wish, and other thoughts, influence what we might consider to be worthwhile. But the more rigorously we examine this complex web of ideas and the more actively we observe and record the evidence of what and how children learn in their playful involvements with the activities devised and resourced in classrooms, the more likely it is that what is offered to children in relation to building their overall ICT competence will have the true dimensions of quality. Quality is essentially something which changes and grows. Like play and players, quality provision demands that teachers build progressively upon existing foundations so that something even more significant emerges.

The teacher

Teachers face the same decision-making processes in using computer software as with any other curriculum resource; that is, how to integrate it smoothly into existing provision in a way which enhances learning. In play, the question becomes how best to achieve the integration of play and imagination into the learning process as a means of encouraging children to be active creators of shared knowledge.

Extending and enhancing learning using ICT

Cameo 3 shows one of the ways in which new technologies can be utilized in classrooms to increase the learning potential of existing successful teaching strategies. The practices associated with imaginative play and early literacy development have been enhanced, and made even more like the real thing by incorporating a laptop. Another simple but very successful approach of this kind was reported by Chadwick (1995). One very popular activity involved children and their families taking home one of a pair of teddy bears for an overnight stay. When the bears came back to school the other children and staff learnt about each visit from the host family by means of verbal accounts, photographs, pictures and sometimes written messages. Each teddy was properly equipped as an overnight guest with toothbrush, bag and other essential items. This was a very successful link for the youngest children between their lives at home and at school. When the school became involved with the National Council for Educational Technology (NCET) laptop project, teddy's visiting bag also contained an inexpensive notepad computer. Parents, children and other helpers began to use this to help the two-way flow of information and develop and foster an interest in ICT. We know of other classes and teachers who have adopted this idea very successfully, making changes to the original idea so that their own existing schemes could be appropriately enhanced. It is not necessary for every message back to school to come in the adult conventional form of writing unless this is part of your learning target. Emergent writing supported by talk conveys quite realistically everything that a class of pupils might need to know about teddy's (or some other hero's) ongoing adventures. Journals such as *Microscope*, in which teachers and others write about their own classroom activities and projects, are always useful sources of inspiration.

Hardware and its play potential

A different approach is to identify a particular piece of technology – for example the fax machine or e-mail system – and analyse what potential it might offer for playful investigations. Boys (1997), in an account of her involvement with part of British Telecom's Gemini project work, gives a delightful description of the ways in which a group of playgroups, a nursery and local infant classes began to use telephone and fax communications to extend their literacy activities by providing a real reason for talk. At first the messages, although numerous and very effective at involving the children in active communication, were largely from members of the children's families. At this point Boys reports: 'The broader community also became involved. In an attempt to extend the project a local garage owner (under promise of secrecy) became our first fax fairy and the children were consequently able to perceive the fax as a tool for communicating beyond the family' (1997: 26). Teachers have often used postal communication and mysterious messages to hook children playfully into the communication game but this was the first account of a more technological approach.

Software and its play potential

Cameo 1 illustrates a very powerful approach to problem solving. Educational adventure games come with supportive directional information for teachers which may require further 'customizing' to meet the learning objectives for a specific class of pupils. Our experience is that playing these types of game works best when integrated into ongoing whole-class plans, rather as a literary text might be.

Adventure games could easily go *on-line* and become shared explorations between two classes of children in the same or different schools, or form the basis for a project involving older and younger pupils working together in a similar manner to that used for book-making or shared reading. Other extensions might include using a computer bulletin board to encourage pupils to seek help from class members in answering questions which have been generated by their project enquiries. These could be addressed to everyone and the teacher and pupils could respond in a 'helpful hint' manner or a 'brainstorming of ideas' way as well as simply answering factual questions. Question-posing is a very important aspect of learning: if you can identify what information you need to help you move forward in your understanding then you are already well advanced in solving your problem. When there is no risk in answering questions, as in the imaginary worlds of Cameos 1 and 3, fellow players will feel able to respond in a lighthearted manner, one which allows for a range of different and even unusual perspectives to be considered – a truly 'mindful' approach to the growth of cognitive ability.

Langer (1997) categorizes 'mindful learning' by a number of characteristics. For example: being able to look at a problem from more than one angle; being able to pick out for oneself something 'new' in any situation and being able to put all kinds of information together into our own categories when we think carefully about a situation (1997: 22–8). Whitebread (1997) makes some rather similar points about children playing with computer adventure games (see the further reading section at the end of this chapter).

Assisting performance

As teachers we can help children play and encourage them to take risks in a number of ways. For example, by:

- ensuring a classroom climate which promotes questioning;
- arranging some means of questions getting responses other than from each other;
- creating opportunities (e.g. time and space) for open-ended exploration;
- structuring exploration by limiting the range of choices to be made (e.g. posing limited challenges: 'Can you achieve this effect using only five key strokes?');
- providing simple challenges for the children to meet ('Devise three questions on mammals which could be answered only by using the CD-Rom we have in class');
- encouraging children to think of ideas to explore in their computer play ('Who can make the longest list of menu suggestions for the "Space monsters' Healthy Eating Book"?';
- ensuring children discuss with others the decisions they made and the reasons for them – being right is not always important, but being able to identify, describe and justify your actions to someone else often helps you to understand your own learning more clearly.

We can encourage children to play with curriculum content in a wide range of areas – for example, line, pattern and form are all important to both art and maths. Constructing shapes, altering their size, creating repeating sequences or generating number and spatial patterns with drawing packages or using 'Roamer'-type approaches all have potential for creative investigations in mathematics. The links between music and computers can be developed by playing with compositional software: transpositions, repeats, reversals and sequences are important to both knowledge domains (Upitis *et al.* 1997). Computer play seems to be particularly effective in promoting developments which teachers might not have expected or anticipated (see Jessel and Hurst 1997).

Quality play

The strength of play lies in its goal-directed nature which ensures that 'giving up' on encountering problems is not an acceptable option. Becoming a skilled key-player requires that the child make progress within play. In each of our cameos, although the play offers valuable learning potential, it is not the same. Development and progression are part of mindful-learning-play in the classroom, nursery or home. Detailed and honest analysis of ICT play will allow us to pinpoint the valuable aspects of activities and indicate how children's learning is being enhanced by each planned opportunity as well as indicating the steps towards progression. Rich play situations offer rich learning and teaching opportunities for decision making, problem solving and the construction of meaningful dialogue.

Observation is the primary means of identifying and analysing the quality dimensions and learning potential of computer play activities, as it is in other forms of learning. If we feel that, as busy classroom practitioners, we don't have time to stand back and observe then perhaps thinking of this activity as a small-scale research project will help. Viewed in this way observation becomes an activity to develop our skills in data collection and analysis – part of the important evidence base which is needed to securely identify what is 'actually' going on in classrooms. Perhaps as teachers we could develop our own knowledge and skill in the use of databases and improve our own ICT competence by collecting, categorizing and recording the outcomes of a number of short observations of each of a small group of pupils 'just playing' with whatever software or hardware appears suitable. 'Findings' could then be exchanged with fellow teachers in our own or another school using 'on-line' facilities to discuss what each of us has discovered, as well any techniques and strategies which have been developed or adapted successfully for any part of the 'research' sequence.

Steps in data collection for assessment in play and ICT use

Observation
Identify and name target children for each observational session. Identify the focus of observation, for example:

- keyboard skills;
- use of specific question forms;
- ability to take and act on advice.

Identify observational method, for example:

- attempt a continuous but brief chronological record of all that happens in a five-minute slot;
- use a predetermined schedule to check use of distance and direction commands in floor turtle operation;
- undertake time sampling – that is, a brief rapid check carried out and recorded at specific times, say every 15 minutes;
- use a pupil tracking sheet within a play session to map the movements of your target child.

Interviews
Interviews with pupils can also be useful. These need not be formal or lengthy but could involve, for example, making a video recording of a play sequence and then discussing with the target child his or her thinking about when she or he did certain things. In Cameo 3, for example, the child could be asked to talk about her reasons for asking a co-player for help with spelling. The use of video is very commonplace in many early years settings and should not be intrusive in its effect on children's play. 'Smiley face' responses to a small number of verbal questions would reveal what children feel about different events. Older pupils might tape-record each other's responses to three key teacher-posed questions, perhaps adding one of their own for the teacher to respond to later. Changes in understanding or confidence will emerge if such information is collected 'before and after' some planned teacher intervention.

Logs and diaries
When kept by pupils these can be really useful as a source of very detailed information about children's learning and thinking processes, especially if these include some indication of why a decision was made.

To analyse such data of children and computer-play teachers should answer questions such as:

- What exactly are children doing (actions and response here)?
- What does this tell me about their understanding (our interpretations here)?
- What are they saying?
- How does this talk enable children to make meaning in this context?
- What could or should the adult do and say? Now or later?

This information provides support for *evidence-based practice* as well as contributing constructively to record keeping. As Chapter 6 will show, factual records from groups of teachers have a place in short-, medium- and long-term planning for pupils developing competence in ICT, and comparisons of effective monitoring of play activities will have considerable staff development potential.

Whatever else this model requires it certainly anticipates an active role in the play process for teachers. The main way to justify play as a legitimate classroom activity is to become actively involved in it, as players, directors or resource providers. Harnessing the power of play to curriculum objectives is well described by Sparrow (1991).

At the beginning of this chapter the two key dimensions of play – its imaginary world dimension and its rule-governed nature – were outlined. Having explored the relationship of play involving computers to identify the central learning strand it seems important to close with a reminder of the danger of the over-intellectualization of play. While play undoubtedly has an enormous contribution to make to cognitive development it is more than this; it has a part to play in the development of affective domains too. There is much that is pleasurable about play and we would be wise not to forget this (Vygotsky 1978).

Summary

This chapter has considered play and technology in a range of settings. It considered how learning can be promoted and enhanced by teachers' identification of clear objectives for play and for the introduction of whatever technological or ICT equipment they have selected.

Recognizing the strengths and demands of play requires the active involvement of the teacher or other adult at various critical points during the process. Children very quickly pick up messages from the hidden classroom agenda and what is not valued by teachers very soon becomes devalued by children. Teachers show, by their careful preparation and planning, the extent to which they see valuable learning within play and ICT. Ongoing interest and involvement in this 'hard fun' is shown by the teacher through a number of strategies:

- careful initial planning and adequate resourcing (including time);
- active, if intermittent, participation in the play;
- interventions as action director or skilful questioner;
- careful observation of learning gains within the play situations;
- recording of assessments made in these contexts.

Points to consider

1 Design an observational schedule for assessing the qualitative dimension of computer play relevant to a year group which would focus either on ICT techniques or processes or the social interactions and language skills required by the play activity you are focusing upon.
2 Draw a schematic floor plan for a thematic play environment in which an actual computer or other technological device would naturally be incorporated. List other resources to complement the thematic focus. Identify five key potential learning outcomes which would be offered by your provision, focusing on one dimension of learning at a time. Computer activity centres have tremendous potential for literacy development.
3 Look through some recent accounts of small-scale classroom research investigations – *Reading Research Quarterly* is a good place to start or publications from organizations such as BECTa (British Educational and Communication Technology agency, formerly NCET). Identify something which you think would lend itself to developing practice in your setting. Note what equipment was used and how it was introduced or arranged in the classroom. Note the way in which the teacher-researcher collected the information and used it to reach conclusions about

the value of the task. Identify any changes you would make if you did something similar in your classroom. Persuade a colleague to join you in 'having a go'. Share everything you do and discover with colleagues at a staff development session and challenge them to join you – offer them some help if they feel they need it. Soon your school will be a true community of quality ICT practioners, and you'll have the evidence to prove it!

Further reading

For a detailed consideration of adventure games within the primary curriculum which includes the potential of specific games see Whitebread (1997). Other valuable sources of information of this type of approach can be found in BECTa (NCET), and the National Association for Teachers of English (NATE) publications in the *IT's English, Accessing English with Computers* series, and also in other subject journals such as *Microscope*, and *Language and Learning*.

3

ICT as a learning tool

Cameo 1

As part of their design technology session three Year 5 children are working at the computer using a CD encyclopaedia to find out about three machines developed in the last 100 years. The CD has several different approaches available for searching and the children are finding their way around, using different sections: 'Let's look at people! Let's look at science!' Although two of the children have never used a CD before, the third child, Kaylee, uses a similar one at home. Her home knowledge helps her make suggestions for approaches which the others follow:

'Let's try a key word!'

'Like what? How do you do that?'

'Oh, I don't know – try "machines", or "inventor".'

Cameo 2

Year 2 children are working on a cluster of computers in the open plan area using an art package selected by the teacher because of its potential for shape manipulation. One boy, David, keeps looking at a repeated pattern on the art display near his machine (see Figure 3.1). In the mathematics lessons his class have been looking at using shapes in different ways, repeating, enlarging and rotating them, creating patterns and tessellations.

David asks the nearby classroom assistant, 'How do I get it to do that? I want to make a pattern like that from that bit of my picture.' The assistant shows him how to outline and copy part of the picture, so that it can be pasted in to make a repeating pattern.

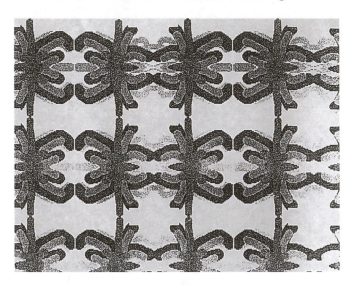

Figure 3.1   A simple reflecting pattern

By the end of the week many children in the class have learned from David how to cut out sections to make repeated patterns. The teacher is very pleased because now they are designing their own patterns and using the mathematical language in ways which are rich in personal meaning.

Cameo 3

A Year 3 class are developing their ideas of number-as-distance-travelled and learning about control through turtle graphics. Some children are using the floor turtle 'Roamer' and entering commands on its integral key pad. Other children are using the Logo program on the computer, doing similar investigations with the screen turtle represented by a small turtle-like symbol on the screen having both position and direction. In either case the turtle is moved by the command *forward* followed by the number of steps it must take in the direction in which it is facing. It can also turn on the spot to point in a different direction. The turning commands (*left* or *right*) are also followed by a number giving the size of the turn in degrees.

Julie and Diane are using the Roamer, working on the problem of sequencing commands to make it cross the room

avoiding an obstacle – a box placed directly in its path. They
have worked out the turtle steps to reach the box and now
need to turn the turtle to move round the box. They have
already tried a turn of 6 degrees, but this had little effect. They
are discussing their actions as they press the buttons on top of
the Roamer.

Julie says, 'Start again and make the turn bigger – clear the
memory.'

Diane presses the keys as she speaks: 'Ok, so that is CM,
CM, to clear the memory . . . forward six . . . left . . . shall we
make it eight?'

'Oh no, it needs to be a lot bigger than that! Try eighteen or
twenty-eight.'

'Twenty-eight . . . GO!'

They both watch as the Roamer approaches the box, stops
and turns a little way to the left.

'It's still not far enough is it?' says Julie. 'Shall I turn
another twenty-eight?' She brings the turtle back to the
starting position and adds the commands *left 28, GO*, and the
two girls watch the Roamer repeat the sequence, this time
turning twice at the box. They both walk across to it and
discuss if another turn is needed to make it clear the edge of
the box.

Cameo 4

Josh, aged 10 years, comes out of class with three of his
classmates for his session on the integrated learning system
(ILS) computers set up in the corner of the hallway. These
computers run teaching programs in mathematics and keep
detailed records for every child using them. Josh and his
classmates have been working on the ILS maths for several
months now and have three sessions every week, each 12
minutes long. The computer system has all the records of what
Josh has attempted and achieved over these months, and uses
this to decide on the next topic for him, and the level at which
to present it. He sits at a computer, ignoring the other boys,
and types in his own personal number. Josh's computer then
goes straight into the mathematical practice where he finished
yesterday, on multiplication of decimals. Each time he gets the
right answer he is congratulated: Well Done! Splendid! Quite
Right! and given another problem. Periodically Josh's class
teacher reviews the pupil ILS records in order to adjust the
medium-term mathematical planning for activities on the
machines and in the classroom.

Introduction

This chapter explores some of the 'learning tools' which children use to find out about things which they need to know, through their interactions with the people and environment around them. By learning tools we have in mind everything – people, machines, processes and talk – which helps to mediate between the learner and the outside world. This chapter also explores how children learn by asking for assistance when they need the information or other help necessary to pursue their own objectives. It suggests that children should be encouraged to continue to link, in a complementary manner, the richness of home learning with that of the school environment. By its very nature, ICT is about making links between the school and the world outside its doors. Teachers have prime responsibility for ensuring that children are supported in developing the strategies and confidence necessary for this kind of learning to take place. They also need to retain pedagogic control of the software, to determine how it should best be used in furthering the children's learning.

The child

Making sense of what computers let us do

The four cameos at the beginning of this chapter show children working with very different types of software. Although each cameo focuses on different learning tasks and activities there are some similarities between them. In Cameo 1 the children are having a first experience of using a new CD, and apparently being very successful with it. In trying to find out about a particular topic they are investigating how the program works and at the same time building an understanding or 'mental model' of how the information is organized on this particular CD. Since Kaylee has used one before, the other children are learning from her and the incomplete knowledge of each of them is improving all the time. This way of learning through interaction with a more knowledgeable 'other' is sometimes described as *assisted performance*. Having someone to help us learn something new will be a familiar experience for most people and is something we all recall from our very earliest days onwards.

This first experience with the CD is largely about learning the techniques for locating the required information within that particular CD. The children are 'playing' with the software in the sense of discovering 'What can I get this to do for me?' This is a positive starting point for their confidence-building but information retrieval activities require much more than simply knowing how to locate data. Children then require more specific targets set within their learning in relation to analysing and abstracting what is useful from within what they have discovered, as we discuss later in the chapter.

The boys working with Kaylee are picking up ideas about the way the CD is organized from Kaylee's suggestions and the response of the program to the various key presses they make. They do not need to ask direct questions but can implicitly test their ideas by trying them out and watching responses. The girls in Cameo 3 are similarly finding out what commands to use by watching the turtle's response. The turtle is acting as the learning tool, and they are sharing ideas and keeping a record of their moves, using the results of each trial to determine the next move. Using this approach, children are learning not only about number as linear or angular displacement, but also about how to make use of the results of trial moves to solve problems in novel situations. In addition they can bring in any other understanding they think might be relevant – for example the knowledge that a left turn will 'undo' a right turn of the same magnitude, maintaining the turtle on a straight course.

In Cameo 2, David needs extra information to achieve what he wants. From observing the display of repeated patterns, and from his knowledge of the program he is using, he guesses correctly that patterns can be made with it. Because he wants to be able to make patterns like those on the wall display, he finds a way to learn how to do it by asking for guidance. He is then able to help other children to do the same. He does this by demonstrating how the menu works and helping his peers to find the appropriate 'cut and paste' commands.

Like David, other children find computer activities highly motivating and work very hard to achieve improved performance and better effects (Cox 1997). When these are shared with others there is an enhancing effect on everyone's learning. As Cameo 2 shows, the social nature of learning does not just affect a child's preferences for working with a specific group, but can set aspirations and expectations for others. We are all influenced by what we see others around us achieving. In David's case a display of work showed him what was possible, and such displays of children's work throughout school serve this purpose very effectively. This model of sharing expertise provides a social context in which the children can grow and develop within their learning community.

ICT work offers a key tool for children to demonstrate not only their knowledge of the computer, as in Cameo 1, but also subject domain knowledge such as mathematics. Hughes (1986) was one of the first to show how children's early experiences of numbers resulted in many different ways of knowing about mathematics which it is only too easy to underestimate in the classroom. The girls in Cameo 3 already have a good understanding of numbers as a forward input, but are still developing their ideas on numbers as an amount of turn. Vaughan (1997) found that when 4-year-old children were given a Roamer to play with they quickly learned how to use their existing knowledge of large numbers for input commands when the small ones they had first selected had so little effect. The children surprised even their teachers who, in this case, had no idea of the pupils' skills with large numbers. Open-ended computer tasks such as those shown in the first three cameos are very valuable in providing opportunities for children to demonstrate their prior knowledge and understanding, and in this way allow home-expertise to become validated within the school situation.

In Cameos 1 and 3 the children had been set clear task objectives, the achievement of which involved experimentation. In contrast David, in Cameo 2, set his own learning objectives and was very successful in creating the type of pattern he had visualized and in linking the art package to the mathematical activities which the class had done. When he was able to share his enthusiasm, his practical skills and his mathematical ideas effectively with the other children, the teacher was delighted. The end result of a number of children creatively linking different curriculum areas for their own purposes was a gratifying conclusion to several days work.

David was successful because he was really determined and knew what effect he wanted to create. All he needed to know was how to use specific aspects of the art package, and help was at hand when he wanted it. Even simple art packages have a wide range of tools and facilities available, particularly relating to form and colour, which can contribute significantly to children's developing appreciation of art. Children do need to be aware of the existence of these possibilities in order to investigate them effectively. It is easy, for example, to show quite young artists how to produce patterns of both regular and irregular shapes and to switch colours over to try out different colour combinations. They also need to be encouraged to experiment to produce particular effects. David learned about these from the displays, but some overt teaching for all the class would have been appropriate in empowering all the children to gain increased subject knowledge and skills.

In Cameo 4 the computer is presenting tasks to Josh in a very directed way. He does not need to seek for information in the closed tasks set, but if he makes a mistake the computer takes him back to an earlier stage in the exercise to remind him of what he has already mastered. This learning model looks very different since, unlike Kaylee, Julie, Diane and David, Josh has no control over or responsibility for what he is doing other than responding to the task he has been allocated, but even here there are some similarities with assisted performance.

The computer tutorial software Josh is using is actually designed to take over the role of training children in elementary number skills. Traditionally this has been a common vision of the role that the computer *ought* to play in education, as a sophisticated electronic tutor with infinite patience and wisdom, setting graded learning tasks. It is a seductive view and one which is increasingly proving popular in highly resourced schools. However, it may only offer us a partial view. At first glance the ILS model of learning seems somewhat closer to the 'passive transmission model' (Ernest 1990), which does not seem to take account of children's broader knowledge or the ways in which mathematical processes may be developed so that they can be used and applied more widely (Boaler 1993). ILS packages offer some valid techniques, but some software systems of this type have been shown to be more effective than others. Many children find them very motivating and appreciate the privacy of the feedback, especially concerning errors they have made (Brown and Underwood 1997). ILS packages are seen as helpful because they:

- take note of the performance of each child and adjust the level of difficulty in the problems offered accordingly;
- provide simple exercises with demonstrated solutions and repeated practice;
- provide report-back facilities for teachers to use when assessing progress.

Crucially, however, ILS packages follow their own agenda and take no cognizance of the richness of children's existing knowledge and cultural experience. Their use must then be 'interpreted' by the teacher and the children's mathematical learning supplemented by more open-ended tasks. The teacher still needs to take overall responsibility to ensure progress. (See Brown and Underwood 1997 for more information and evaluation of ILS.)

The context

Presentation of the learning task

Within ILS the task presentation is determined by the computer, but this is not the case with other ICT tools. In Cameo 1 the task was set up by the teacher, challenging the children to find out about inventions in the last 100 years using the new CD-Rom. As a first experience with the CD encyclopaedia this would be sufficient to allow exploration of the different facilities. It is an open-ended approach in which neither the children nor the teacher know entirely what is going to happen. The learning context would have been different if the teacher had given the children a set of instructions to follow. The context in which children work depends greatly on the way in which the task is presented to them.

By exploring Cameo 1 we can consider the advantages of different approaches to meeting a new piece of software – in this case the CD-Rom – for Year 5 children. We suggest three possible presentations:

- Approach A: provide the minimum instruction to get into the program, and then set up a general, open-ended challenge, e.g. 'Find out what you can about scientific inventions in the first half of this century, with a recommendation that they make a note about what moves they make.

Table 3.1   Three approaches to locating information

Open-ended	Overview	Detailed instructions
Children can demonstrate what they already know	Children know where to start	Children know what buttons to press
They can make discoveries	They can make discoveries	They only find out what they were told to find out
They can't go wrong, there is no right or wrong	They should not get lost	They should not get lost unless they press the wrong button
This is providing meaningful learning	The learning may be meaningful	The learning is unlikely to be meaningful
More likely to be able to use the system again	More likely to be able to use the system again	Unlikely to know how to use the system again except for an identical search
May waste time trying to find ways in	May find instructions too complicated	May feel they have failed if they do not get the right answer

- Approach B: provide an overview of the three main searching strategies when using the CD. Explain how one can link to another and how the backward and forward arrows work. Set a few specific questions with suggestions of possible search routes, e.g. 'Who was Louis Pasteur?' (select the 'People' icon and then use the alphabetic index); 'What sort of animals did the Peruvian Incas use?' (select the 'Map of the World', then select 'South America' from it).
- Approach C: provide detailed instructions, e.g. to find 'French scientists' click on the 'People' icon, choose 'Scientist' from the next list, etc.

These approaches are summarized in Table 3.1.

With Approaches A and B the children should be learning how to use the CD for any investigation, and how the information is stored in it. In Approach B the children may forget some of the information and there would be a need to choose the difficulty level with which they could cope. In Approach C children may only be learning how to look up particular types of information, for instance about people. If asked about something else they may not know how to instigate the search. Another problem with this approach is that if anything goes wrong – say they click in the wrong place – it may result in pupils getting completely lost and having to start again, causing valuable time to be lost and potentially creating a degree of technological frustration. Following instructions tends to make commands less memorable and having to cope with a detailed worksheet, as well as the screen, could prove distracting. The age and experience of the children, however, needs to be taken into account. Younger children using a program for the very first time may be more comfortable with Approach C. Progression in this case must involve gaining sufficient confidence to begin a new search with only an approximate idea about exactly how to do this.

Sharing solutions

When small groups of children have experienced navigating round the CD encyclopaedia using Approaches A or B then learning could be further developed if everyone was encouraged to compare notes about the ways in which they each acquired their information and explored solutions using the CD. It is in this way that children learn from their peers and have their own learning consolidated. Ideas about *efficient* and *inefficient* approaches could be developed between them, so that they could all be helped to understand how the information is arranged. They could draw diagrams on paper to show the connections between different screens, and so develop mental models to help in future encounters to access and utilize the information.

Teachers also need to remember all that has been learnt about the way in which printed information texts work and the ways in which children can be helped to access information constructively (see Neate 1991). We now know so much about constructing and using printed information texts that to have software designers take us back to earlier, poorly organized, types of text such as those found in older information books, even though the information as they offer it on the screen appears to be visually exciting, would be a retrograde step. Since so much of education in the future will be related to obtaining, using, manipulating and evaluating information, knowing how we develop mental models of the way material might be arranged logically for rapid and easy retrieval is going to be a lifelong skill worth us all learning.

Techniques and processes in ICT

Developing sophisticated retrieval skills takes time, but progression in all ICT skills is something which should be built into each child's development throughout school. The skills we are talking about here are at two different levels which we will call *techniques* and *processes*. Techniques are related to the actual program being used – which menu to use, where to click, which keys to press to achieve certain effects, etc. Processes reflect what can be achieved by using particular techniques – for instance, the development of repeating patterns in art, or the editing and redrafting of a piece of text.

Techniques are generally specific to a particular piece of software and type of machine, and only of any value while that software and computer are in use, though there are moves towards more standardization in the design of software. However, *process* knowledge and understanding is durable over a longer timespan, and represents truly transferable learning. Both processes and techniques are required for learners to make good use of these technological tools in their learning. Techniques should be taught in such a way as to keep children attached to the processes they facilitate. Given experiences of using these together with a range of software, children's future learning should be considerably enhanced.

Teachers should integrate the teaching of ICT skills within each curriculum area. The *processes* should always activate pupils to learn and apply the *techniques* when they can see some practical application for them – processes should *drive* techniques. This was the case in the first three cameos: the children were all trying to develop processes to meet their task objectives, and 'found' the techniques as they were required. Meaningful learning arises when there is a reason for learners to want to know something or where there is a desire to reach a particular goal. So, for instance, when first learning to search a CD-Rom encyclopaedia the search should be linked to a current curriculum focus, related to geography, RE or another subject area. The particular direction of the search could come from a set of questions generated by a group of children arising from their topic, or from cross-curricula investigations.

If we think of word processing in English as an example of a 'group of ICT processes' we can see that children need to be taught how to extend their ICT process knowledge about drafting, redrafting and editing their texts on any machine using any word processor (remember that some machines are more 'child-friendly' than others). In order to carry out the ICT processes, children will also need to learn the *techniques* (that is, which keys to press and when) which are required by any specific program. When they know about both elements they will be able to move their text around within a document (a process commonly called 'cut and paste'). But the overall learning purpose of extending their ability to communicate in writing through the use of a word processor should always be kept in sight, and this is discussed later in this chapter.

The teacher

Encouraging learning display

Much learning-enhancing software involves an element of experimentation. The learning tools in Cameos 1–3 show an analytic approach to learning which asks children to think about what happens and when changes might be useful. Teachers, by challenging children to produce particular effects, can encourage this analytic approach using a wide range of software.

Initially the teacher's role in this 'assisted performance' will be to observe carefully and allow the children to investigate and puzzle things out for themselves. This allows the children's independent learning to be recognized and encouraged, and also allows them to realize that their efforts are valued by their teachers. Such autonomous learning is also highly motivating to children (Pollard *et al.* 1994) and the fact that computers offer such control opportunities may account for the fact that IT is found to be the most popular school activity among 7-year-old pupils (West *et al.* 1997).

Teacher directed approach

While open-ended activities, where children learn through trial and error, are important both in establishing what children already know and can do, and in enabling them to direct their own learning, there are times when it is important and appropriate for children to be *taught* particular computer skills. In this way the teacher can ensure that the children make progress using particular software and so add new tools to their repertoire for approaching open-ended problems. Demonstrations to the whole class or to a large group offer useful and efficient strategies to be followed up by children engaging in some purposeful activity using these tools while pursuing their own aims. They could, for instance, widen their creative use of paint tools by employing the 'spray gun' to develop shadow effects on their individual work once this has been demonstrated, or be taught how to build *procedures* in turtle graphics. Once they have mastered the sequencing of direct commands children can be set appropriate challenges developing geometric patterns using these procedures. (See appendix for further information on Logo procedures.)

The teacher orchestrates the learning experience with ICT learning tools by:

- introducing new computer tasks;
- setting challenges;
- providing supportive intervention when required;
- making time for consolidation of the children's learning;
- teaching new skills to ensure progress is maintained;
- setting up more advanced challenges, etc.

Introducing and supporting new software

Introducing new computer applications needs to be done sensitively so that children can all make a good start. A Roamer makes an excellent introduction to turtle graphics as the movements of this three-dimensional object can be copied by children. They can progress to using screen turtles when they are confident with a Roamer's moves. Equally, the facilities of a word processor can be quite complex without the additional complications of using the full keyboard. Teachers can simplify the introductory stages of word processing in two different ways.

First, they can offer support to young writers by providing an on-screen word bank relating to missing or important words in order to reduce the spelling or typing demands of the task. Children can begin to understand the word processor's potential utility for altering page layout, text size and style, without, at this stage, having to concern themselves too much with finding letters on the keyboard or remembering too many spellings. Many simplified programs with on-screen word banks and alternative keyboards are available for young children, beginners and children with learning difficulties. Chapter 6 addresses this issue and the appendix contains more details on simplified approaches.

Second, when focusing on drafting, redrafting and editing skills some very thought-provoking work can be done using text files which teachers have prepared. These will allow pupils to develop 'cut and paste' skills at the same time as they read and analyse the text and develop logical and analytical thinking. In history, English or science, activities might include:

- sequencing events in a text file chronologically or logically;
- supporting arguments, e.g. by highlighting words and phrases in a descriptive passage about imaginary monsters which suggest that the monsters are really quite friendly;
- deciding which of the steps taken would lead to a fair test in a science investigation and cutting and pasting these into a different document.

The teacher's key to deciding which type of approach is appropriate to use in any particular situation is to focus on the objectives for the children's learning as well as the context in which the computers are being used.

Pedagogic control and the choice of software

Teachers always have overall control of what goes on in their classrooms, but with the introduction of more and more computers there may be a tendency to use programs somewhat unquestioningly. This is essentially abdicating our responsibility to the software developer. In Cameo 4, Josh's teacher is working *with* the software developer to maximize the system's effectiveness. When the classroom and the computer work are closely linked and the teacher is able to use the individual pupil records produced by ILS packages for ongoing planning, then these systems are most productive in mathematics (Brown and Underwood 1997). The teacher is maintaining pedagogic control in this case.

We know far more about education than software developers and we also know more about the learning needs of the children in our care. If learning is thought of as including discussion, negotiation and children reporting their activities, as it often is, we as teachers have a central role in establishing the quality of the learning environment because of the influence we have over:

- the organization of the class;
- the themes and topics developed;
- the software and other learning tools provided.

In Cameo 2, David made the link between the mathematical work in the classroom and the art package tools. The teacher here is developing a theme by providing opportunities in different curriculum areas and activities which relate to the focus on shapes. The exploration is open-ended, but the support is there in the visual environment, through adult support and the facilities provided by the program. Pedagogic control here exemplifies all three areas of control listed above. In Cameo 3, the teacher has retained control by defining the task, although they have not specified the way in which it should be carried out.

Many worthwhile computer activities, particularly those using general learning tools such as word processors, art packages, databases or information resources (CD-ROMs and the Internet), are not one-off experiences but programs which will be revisited continually throughout the children's school careers. We need to ensure that these repeated experiences are truly progressive and incrementally demanding as children develop their ICT skills.

Returning to our earlier example of word processing to illustrate this point, it is important to ensure that children develop their knowledge of word processors in a systematic way and one which reflects important aspects of their learning in English within the relevant key stage. What is important is that pupils are given opportunities to create written texts using ICT for a range of purposes and using a variety of forms. Children working in English using a word processor should be involved in producing text at the various stages of the writing process from initial planning through draft and revision stages to the point at which their text is ready for 'publication' – that is, presentation to its intended audience.

Over a period of time, and using a number of different pieces of writing, an example of every stage of the process could be collected to show how the writers are dealing with ongoing decision making. Extra printouts or photocopies of 'work in progress' could be annotated by the children, with the help of the teacher if necessary, to show how or when they carried out the planning stage using ICT, or how another piece had undergone 'reordering' during the drafting stage. Such records can indicate the children's level of awareness about their chosen *form of writing*, the *intended purpose* of their text and the *audience* they are creating it for.

Responses to feedback from writing partners or the teacher can be shown at the revision and proofreading phases which will reveal ways in which children have developed their strategies concerning punctuation and spelling. It is not necessary for each stage of every text to be accessed using the word processor and it is often not possible because of scarcity of resources. Teachers must decide which aspect of the writing process is most useful within any given piece of a child's work.

It is useful to begin by allowing everyone to have a turn in using the word processor for the planning stage, as this allows children to share and discuss their first thoughts about the kind of information which needs to be included in their piece of writing. In a narrative, even the youngest writers can respond simply in one or two words to the key questions:

- Who is your story about?
- Where is it going to happen?
- When is it going to happen?
- What is going to happen to the people in your story?
- How does everyone feel about these events?

This first planning draft will be developed later, possibly as a group story or as an oral account (Wray and Medwell 1989).

Subsequently, children could work on other stages, such as drafts developed using more traditional writing tools or pictorial planners. If resourcing permits, word processors allow for drafting and editing experiences of a type offered by no other tool. Producing a final, polished copy is just one, and possibly the least developmentally useful way, of using word processors to develop both ICT and writing skills together. The powerful impact of a well-presented text on both its writer and the intended audience should not be underestimated. It is always a real thrill to see one's writing looking 'like a real book'. Word processors are key writing tools, as any professional writer will readily acknowledge. Children need to become comfortable and competent users from their earliest developmental stage as writers with a message to communicate, but this does not mean that every stage of every piece of writing needs to involve ICT. Rather, a range of different ways of developing text should be explored with children.

Pupils' contribution to assessment

The teacher's assessment of skills and progress will be made by observing pupils working on the computer, but the pupils can also take some responsibility for ticking off tasks, on check sheets, that they can accomplish unaided. It is obviously important that, once they have achieved a certain level of skill, children maintain it by regular use of ICT. Even experienced teachers find that they forget the correct procedures required in some computer tasks if they do not practise them regularly. Once children are able to open the programs they want, save their work and print out what is necessary, they should be expected to do this independently each time they use the computer. By the end of Key Stage 2 pupils will be expected to take more responsibility for their computer use, including making their own decisions about when and where it is appropriate to use particular applications.

Summary

This chapter started by suggesting that children be encouraged to make use of their prior knowledge in school and outlined how they can be given the opportunity to develop this by teachers providing open-ended tasks within computer work. The computer context is seen as a significant part of the overall classroom context and tasks and activities within ICT are set up and controlled by the teacher who takes overall pedagogic responsibility. The teacher must ensure progression in the children's ICT experience and skills development. This is an issue to which we will return to in Chapter 6.

Points to consider

1 Below are some suggestions for the way general computer skills may be developed, for use in quick checklists of skills development.

General computer handling skills

Simple level:
- switch on;
- load a program;
- use the mouse, keyboard, overlay keyboard;
- save work;
- print out.

Moderate level:
- use e-mail;
- browse the Internet from the home page;
- understand about filing and directories.

Advanced level:
- use peripheral input devices (scanner, camera and video input);
- use search facilities efficiently on the Internet;
- understand the different forms in which information can be stored (data types) and the interchange and transfer possibilities between them.

Do you agree with these? At what stage in their education would you expect children to achieve these levels?

2 Try to produce your own skills lists for the following:

- communication skills;
- information retrieval skills;
- data handling skills.

3 What important ICT *processes* are facilitated by these skills? What contexts could you use to introduce or develop these skills, to bring out the use and transferability of these processes?

Further reading

The School Curriculum and Assessment Authority's (SCAA) 1997 document, *Expectations in Information Technology at Key Stages 1 and 2*, gives general guidance on what children should be expected to achieve at the end of each key stage. This document is written using processes as exemplification – for example, at the end of Year 2 children are expected to use a computer-based paint package to produce a picture. Other agency documents have provided further exemplification. Booklets provided by BECTa and QCA (Qualifications and Curriculum Authority), as well as articles in many teachers' journals such as *Child Education* and *Microscope*, offer further useful reading in this area.

4

Managing learning

Cameo 1

Two 8-year-old girls are working at the side of the classroom on Logo. They have a card with suggested patterns and pictures with a Christmas theme they might draw. The teacher has designed this activity to challenge the pupils to use a variety of different angles and to appreciate how symmetry can be simply produced by changing left and right turns. The rest of the class are working individually in their maths groups. A few boys keep walking past to look at the screen and exchange a few words with the girls, some five or six times. The girls are getting a bit annoyed with them but don't want to draw attention to themselves. The teacher comes to see the girls and is a bit surprised when they show her their creation. They explain that the Christmas tree went wrong, so they turned it into a star pattern. The teacher questions them about the processes through which they came to complete their picture and is happy that they have demonstrated a clear understanding of symmetry, and commends them for not giving up and for developing their idea even if it is a bit different. The girls leave the computer, tick the chart on the wall to say which card they have used, tell the next pair of children it is their turn, and go back to their other maths work.

Cameo 2

Picture a computer lab with 16 computers arranged around three sides, all with hard disks and a database program on-screen. Nine-year-old children are working two or three to a machine. They have collected information on sheets of paper about their favourite toys, and those of their grandparents, under a set of different headings (name of toy, type of toy, year when it was used, material it was made of, and so on). The children are typing this information from the sheets onto the screen. The teacher walks round answering questions and ensuring that the papers are passed around, so that each group can type in other sets of data.

After 20 minutes the teacher stops the class. By this time most groups have five or six records entered. The teacher reminds them how they can interrogate the file and how to draw graphs from the data to illustrate significant answers. Although the records are still far from complete she asks them to practise using these database tools on their six records to find the most popular toy of each generation, if there are any toys liked by both generations, and to discuss possible reasons for their findings. Most of the groups are able to do this, after one or two false starts, and the teacher targets help on some of the less confident groups. The more able children quickly complete these queries and go on to think up some more questions of their own and discuss which graphs best illustrate their findings. By the following week the teacher will have ensured that the rest of the data has been entered, checked and copied to all the machines so that all the class can use the complete data set to look for patterns, hypothesizing about toys 50 years ago and today.

Cameo 3

Three children are working in a quiet area equipped with two multimedia computers assisted by Mrs Hayes, a member of the special needs support team. All three children have learning difficulties. They are contributing to the production of an on-line school prospectus which their class is creating. This is to be shown on a big monitor in the hall during the open evening for the parents of children transferring from the infant school.

Toni, Seth and Adam spent the last session taking photos with the digital camera. They took pictures of the school buildings, playground, wilderness area, and each other, and have now plugged the camera into the back of the computer to review their photos. Mrs Hayes talks to them about the photos and they readily decide on the main school pictures to use. They note down carefully which photos will be included in the prospectus but they all feel it would be a good idea to have their own photos in as well, so that the new children will recognize some familiar faces when they arrive. Mrs Hayes suggests that they could also work on pages about themselves; they happily agree.

Toni and Seth save the school pictures on one machine, and Adam then takes the camera to work on the other computer to start his own multimedia page. He pastes in his photo. 'What shall I write?' he asks.

'Your name and age,' suggests Toni.

'Or your favourite football team,' offers Seth.

'No,' says Adam, 'I'll do the things I like in school.'

'That is a good idea,' says Mrs Hayes. 'Shall we check the words in your word bank?'

This is so popular that on open day one computer is set up with the school on-line prospectus welcoming visitors to the school, and another runs a carousel with many individual children's pages which include their portraits, with a sentence or two which they have each created.

Introduction

This chapter looks at the management of learning. While all three elements of child, context and teacher are very important, on this occasion we want to start by focusing on the context because we want to highlight the way in which teachers and adults create contexts of learning in a variety of ways. This view of contexts as not *only* physical spaces is important if learning is seen as having social and interactive elements, as we will demonstrate.

We begin by considering 'context' in terms of the way the word is used and of how context-related terms relate to one other at a practical level. We make a distinction between physical contexts, or settings, and learning contexts, including social and curriculum dimensions.

The teacher in this chapter is considered as the manager of learning with, and in, ICT. Teachers' understandings develop as well as those of the children. This section includes aspects of decision making, preparation, presentation, and assessment.

The child is seen as a very active participant in the learning process. In this section we look at how children interpret and carry out the tasks set by the teacher.

The context

The learning context

As the cameos show, learning can take place in very different places. These three examples are taken from in and around classrooms. There are many other places where children learn effectively but for the moment let's see what is important about the contexts or places we have described. Sometimes, as we have seen, the same word can be used in different ways and the meaning of it can change. Alternatively, people may use several words interchangeably. *Setting, context* and *environment* are some of the words which suffer from these complications. It seems that each of them can be used to describe or talk about:

- the actual physical space in which children are working (e.g. classroom or special lab);
- home, school or club (e.g. something which is part of a wider framework);
- the subject area of the curriculum to which the activity children are engaged in mainly relates (e.g. history, maths or English);
- the way in which children are allowed to behave in order to accomplish their learning (e.g. talking, laughing and sharing ideas, or working in silence);
- the way in which the teacher and the children relate to each other and the activity which is being undertaken.

It is important to consider all of these meanings when making decisions about the ways in which children's learning is to be profitably promoted. Starting with the first idea of deciding about the spaces in which children and teachers work with computers, we can see that our three cameos are very, very different. In many ways decisions about the place in which computers are used influence other items in the list above.

We are using the word *setting* to describe the physical location of the computer. In our three cameos, one setting was a purpose-built computer laboratory within a school (Cameo 2), and the others were part of the general teaching space. The teacher will be involved in deciding where to put computers within the classroom, but whole school decisions (discussed in Chapter 6) may determine how the computers are shared throughout the school.

We will use the word *context* in various ways, generally involved with learning as both social and curriculum elements.

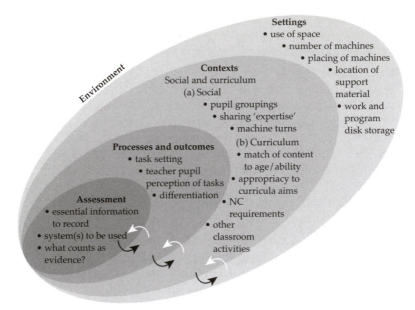

Figure 4.1 A classroom interpretation of the meanings of 'context'

For example, in Cameo 1 a pair of friends are working on solving a joint problem which gives a collaborative social context. The curriculum context is within the mathematics of shape.

The general ambiance of the classroom provides the backdrop to the children's activities – that is, the shared understanding of what constitutes acceptable behaviour which is developed between the teacher and children, exemplified by the level of formality, talk and movement. This constitutes the *environment* within which the learning is situated and may be altered by the inclusion of computer activities within the classroom, but will not be the main focus of attention.

Figure 4.1 shows the 'nesting' of different dimensions of *context*, taking a socio-cultural view of learning which recognizes that it is impossible in the real world to separate out the contributory elements of this process. Although some attempt has been made to use slightly different words for each of the layers shown, it is important to stress that each of these has some effect on every other. Any change in any part of the system has a knock-on effect on every other, so, for example, if the National Curriculum requirements change for ICT then assessment procedures and the use of space may also change. Equally if the number of machines changes, then this will cause changes to occur in the way pupil groupings are arranged, and differentiation may be easier. The layers are rather like those complicated Chinese boxes or building toys given to babies, which drive tidy-minded adults wild when they are rushing to clear them away! Although we have selected this method of displaying the organization of our ideas, it would be just as reasonable to reconstruct them as a tower, each resting on another and each representing whatever ideas seem most important to you. The main point we want to make is that it is very important to take into account the various embedded layers of settings, context and environment when thinking about children's learning. If you can envisage the box layers we have described here, then this presents a picture of what is a very important and key Vygotskian idea. This idea of embedding is much more widely accepted now by educationalists and psychologists. The notion that the impact of these layers makes a big difference to what children learn from the situations they find themselves in at home, school and elsewhere is quite widespread. Donaldson's (1978) research on natural settings for testing what children know and can do, and other work on reading (e.g. Heath 1983; Kress 1997) are very good examples.

The classroom climate

Figure 4.1 shows aspects of learning situations that teachers must consider within each layer. At the outer layer of our model the environment or 'climate of the classroom' exerts an important influence on all the activities which occur there. The rules and procedures which govern classroom life affect profoundly the experiences of all those who find themselves a part of that particular 'knowledge-building community'. How is this climate created? Clearly the wider societal issues such as the overall philosophy of the school, regional and national policy, parental expectations and other outside influences exert great pressure on teachers and children but within this general framework it is these people who construct the reality of day-to-day life. The basic building blocks of this are the relationships developed by the teacher with the children as well as those existing and developing between the children themselves and the talk and actions which form the outward manifestation of development (Edwards and Mercer 1987).

Table 4.1 Strengths, weaknesses and opportunities provided by different computer arrangements

	Strengths	*Weaknesses*	*Opportunities*
1 or 2 machines per class	Cheap Fits with group work Flexible time allocation Part of class project Easy to differentiate tasks	Infrequent use Provides distraction for other pupils Difficult to use during whole-class activities Teacher needs to repeat instructions	Pupil can choose when to use an application Additional support and access to the curriculum can be provided for children with special educational needs Teacher can demonstrate within the classroom
Multiple machines in one room	Only one introduction required All pupils get the same information Less distraction All have the same recorded computer time Machines and software ready for the pupils	Expensive Inflexible time slots Difficult to differentiate tasks for different pupils Technical demands on teacher come at the same time	Peer tutoring Can practise IT skills, e.g. touch typing, loading and saving More opportunity for computer use

The setting

Within the classroom environment the physical organization of the room affects what goes on in it. In particular, most computers are large, significant objects whose position needs to be carefully considered. Two of our cameos illustrate the most commonly found arrangement of one or two machines in a classroom, or in a shared space close by, while the other exemplifies an increas-

ingly popular approach – a computer suite. Whole school decisions may determine the availability of computers and the policies on their use, however we suggest that it is still useful to
reflect upon the advantages of different computer settings. Table
4.1 shows a quick approach to such an analysis.

Other aspects of physical planning, apart from the rooms in
which ICT equipment is sited, have to be decided by the class
teacher. These involve the use of space, provision of support
materials for the children and placing of machines with respect
to the screen orientation.

It is important to achieve the most effective placing of machines,
in order to ensure that there is nothing to put children off using
them (such as needing to move them, or to search round for
disks before they can be used). It is also important to make the
best use of space, particularly in overcrowded classrooms. Clearly,
the primary consideration will be that of safety and many older
buildings in particular have very few, and often inconveniently
sited, sources of power. Long leads and trailing wires must be
avoided at all costs and common sense as well as safety regula-
tions would suggest that certain combinations of activities including water, sand and paint might best be kept apart!

As already indicated we will say more about the setting and
context when considering the role of the teacher and the child.

The teacher

Teachers have many decisions to make in relation to each of the
layers depicted in Figure 4.1. This decision-making process has a
recurring sequential pattern which can be seen as unfolding in
the manner shown in Figure 4.2. All the elements of Bennett's
(1994: 64) cycle need consideration in relation to ICT but in this
section we are most concerned with the implementation, presentation and assessment dimensions.

Each of the cameos has many positive elements. In Cameo 1
the teacher has developed an active learning situation. She has:

• the computer and printer up and running with Logo within a
  maths class;
• groups of children organized to use the computer in turn;
• suggested designs for the children to work towards, with the
  final choice and approach left to them;

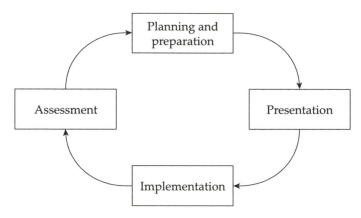

Figure 4.2 The planning cycle
Source: Bennett (1994).

- an informal timing system generally based on completion of two or three designs;
- a recording system working with a tick chart and folders of printouts.

The teacher also has clear expectations of what the children should be learning, though the girls may have been slightly less clear on this point. Although presented in a topical theme associated with Christmas the teacher was primarily interested in the mathematical learning opportunities here, whereas the girls interpreted the task rather more in terms of actual tree design. In taking time to assess their work informally before they returned to their other mathematics work the teacher was able to resolve the confusion in a satisfactory manner. It is all too common to find that children do not understand the purpose of the work they are asked to do (Bennett 1994) and in this instance it would have been better all round to check that the girls really understood what was essential and what was optional about the set task.

Cameo 2 illustrates a completely different kind of teaching approach where the teacher is working with the whole class. Positive points about this presentation and implementation of learning tasks are that:

- all the computers are set up to run the database project;
- this is an integral part of their history/technology project;

- the whole class are working on the computers in small friend-ship groups;
- children have all their own data on paper and are clear about how to enter it into the computer;
- there is a clear focus to the lesson on developing technical skills to cope with the database;
- differentiation is provided by supporting the slower pupils and allowing the more able ones to work at their own rate on a further selection of open-ended tasks.

Here there is evidence that the teacher has planned this session, as part of an overall cross-curricular scheme, to give all the children experience of entering their data onto the computer and to gain some familiarity with the technical aspects of the database. In the following sessions the children will use these skills to focus on the questions which can be asked and answered about toys over the generations, furthering their knowledge of primary source materials and historical enquiry skills.

In Cameo 3 the class teacher and support teacher together have provided:

- a quiet, supported working environment for the children with learning difficulties, while still engaging them in a whole-class project;
- a high profile activity (providing photographs for the pro-spectus) which is excellent for their motivation and self-esteem;
- freedom to allow them to develop their own initiatives;
- extra adult support and time to ensure success.

While the classroom cameos are largely concerned with the presentation and implementation elements of the development cycle, they also reveal something of the planning which has already taken place and have implications for the assessment which is required. Learning with the computer brings in additional essential aspects of managing the learning, including:

- the physical organization of the machines;
- the choice and setting up of the software;
- the curriculum organization of the learning context;
- the social organization of the children;
- the task organization and timing;
- the recording/assessment/evaluation system.

Teachers' personal learning in ICT

As well as coming to terms with all the many dimensions of their teaching situation, teachers also have to become familiar with a range of software and understand how best to relate it to the curriculum and to the children's needs. Here it has been recognized that teachers themselves move through a developmental process in their own understanding about classroom computer use. Underwood (1996) outlines a chronological sequence in the development of this understanding about the management of learning and the use of ICT. This, she feels, reflects a move from a position in which ICT is slotted into traditional teaching sequences towards one reflecting a complete change of curriculum emphasis through new possibilities. Underwood's chronology is summarized below, showing the gradual move from low to high demand on the teacher.

- *Packages making minimal demands on the teacher and pupil's ICT capability or skills.* Short, drill and practice programs or simple picture packages are often used here, bearing no relationship to other classroom activities. They can too easily become time-fillers to occupy children, or worse, to reward the faster workers, and have little merit or educational value.
- *Packages selected to support planned work and fit in with the existing curriculum. ICT would be rejected if there was no relevant software to hand.* As in Cameo 2: the database program was selected to fit in with the planned historical topic to enable graphs to be drawn contrasting the popularity of old and new toys. Subject-specific programs, such as simulations and some adventure games (see Chapter 2) are often used when there is an exploitable match between curriculum work and the software content. There is some educational merit in taking this approach and it allows teachers with few ICT skills to begin to appreciate what can be done. As teachers become more familiar with the programs they begin to see the limitations of the standard approach provided or suggested by the software writer, and want to take more active control over their teaching. As a result they move on to using the computer as a tool.
- *Computer as a tool. This places greater demands on the teacher for ICT skills, classroom organization and time management, and involves planning, integrating and reviewing the learning taking place.* This is happening in Cameo 1, where the logo work was designed

to complement the mathematical shape work undertaken by the rest of the class, and in Cameo 3 where the multimedia design facilities are being used to the full to support the curriculum demands.

• *Core curriculum content delivered through multimedia technology.* Making full use of the Internet and computer-based knowledge sources, giving experienced pupils considerable autonomy in their computer use, orchestrated and supported by the teacher.

The teacher's role

Setting the tasks: processes and outcomes
The teacher has three main responsibilities in setting tasks using computers:

1 ensuring that the computer work extends the learning opportunities of the specific curriculum domain;
2 setting clearly-focused objectives for the ICT tasks;
3 ensuring that the children understand the objectives and their role in attaining them.

In planning each ICT task the teacher needs to consider how it fits in with other related classroom activities, so that it is both meaningful to the children and meets specified learning objectives within that curriculum area. In Cameo 1 the work on angles and reflection that the class were doing was nicely complemented by the logo activities, and the teacher was clear in what she was looking for in the children's work.

The timings within tasks are also crucial: children need to spend most of the working session on the central focus of the learning activity rather than the early preparatory stages. In Cameo 2 the class were working in the computer lab for a fixed amount of time, so the teacher did not wait for all children to finish the data-entry task, but focused on developing familiarity with how the database worked after just a few entries had been made. Data entry itself is of limited educational value once the children understand the way it works and have come to appreciate that the information in the database is the same as that they have personally collected. This sense of 'ownership' is very important, but can usually be gained after keying-in five or six records. The children then need experience in 'playing' with the small set of data to learn how the program operates. Before the next session the teacher can ensure that the full set of data is entered, and the children can then all work on that and develop the graphs to illustrate the key features of the changes in toys over the years, concentrating on the historical questions rather than how the program works (see also Pratt 1995).

Presentation
Having planned the tasks and the place and purpose of ICT within them as well as considered other important dimensions such as differentiation, timing and organization, how the children are going to work in groups and take turns on the computer, it only remains for the teacher to present these to the children. The ways in which this can be done vary from simple instructions to a detailed discussion of what needs to be done together with some discussion of why the 'doers' are doing it, especially if misunderstandings such as that in Cameo 1 are to be avoided. Not being clear about what is important in a task can be very confusing; knowing that alternative solutions are acceptable is very empowering to learners.

The importance of what is to be done can be very much influenced by the way the teacher sets the task for the children. (Just tape-record yourself a few times if you really want to know what you are stressing. One of the authors of this book did this, and subsequently banned the word 'carefully' from her vocabulary!) Equally, the children's perception of what it is they are required to do can have a very profound influence on their efforts and the learning which takes place. Staff rooms echo to teachers' tales in respect of amusing misunderstandings. Work cards, in the form of challenges or problems to be solved (as in Cameo 1) may have a place here, and, when tasks involve using a relatively less well-known computer program, help cards for operating the software could also be provided. Whether their response to the task is assessed in any way, and on what criteria, also directly effects the way in which the children will set about completing it.

Computers are still something of a scarce resource in many schools and the demands of satisfactory progression in ICT require teachers to provide a wide range of experiences for children. For the foreseeable future, teachers will probably also need to have some kind of rolling programme and recording system for ICT, to ensure that children get the experience required to develop positive attitudes and competence. Record systems which work best are those which 'best fit' the purposes for which they are required. Keeping records of individual's ICT development, if not already part of existing systems, probably only requires additions or amendments to existing records.

The child

Children's participation

Vygotskian views emphasize a very strong role for the adult in managing a learning situation. They would however, also have a clear view of the learner as an active participant in this process, making important decisions about, and controlling, their own learning. This is true even of direct instructional situations involving older children. Table 4.2 shows how we have analysed our cameos to indicate the degree of autonomy children have using different programs. (A modest degree of autonomy is indicated by the cross-tick.)

Table 4.2   Children's autonomy when using computer programs: an analysis of Cameos 1–3

Choices	Cameo 1	Cameo 2	Cameo 3
What to do	✔	✗	✓
When to do it	✗	✗	✗
When to finish	✓	✗	✓
Way to start it	✓	✗	✓
Who to work with	✗	✔	✔
How to share tasks	✓	✓	✓

In Cameos 1 and 3 the children were able to work with a high degree of autonomy on the computer tasks. While some children find a lack of clear guidance challenging, most children respond well to being given the freedom to go about a task in their own way, especially when they know that the teacher has high expectations of them. This is an experience too often lacking for children like Adam, Seth and Toni (Cameo 3) who have special educational needs, but the use of technology (the digital camera and the computer in this case) can provide a safe educational context for their self-directed work.

Children's space

It is essential that children are given sufficient space to allow adequate access to the computer. Not only does the group need to work comfortably, but they also need space for storing those resources which necessarily accompany ICT work. Writing materials for the children to make notes and plans as they work on programs, as well as help sheets to enable them to gain their independence in machine management, are essential. They may also need disks for programs or storage of their work.

For continuity and progression in children's ICT work it is essential that they can return to something they have produced earlier to modify, extend or adapt it. Group work disks or hard-disk space accessible to children working independently greatly facilitates this. Pupil responsibility and independence can be developed throughout their primary years and the level of demands which is to be placed on them at any stage in this process is one of the whole school decisions which feature in Chapter 6.

Even the youngest of children in school can be taught to load programs and save work, and may do so with the help of pictorial guides, as many children have demonstrated at home. However it is unfair to *expect* children to come to school with this knowledge. All of them need to be shown gradually how the system will operate in school so that they clearly understand what they are expected to do for themselves and when they should ask the teacher for help. Where laptops are used, efficient, manageable systems need to be in place to enable issuing, battery charging and printing to be achievable by children on their own or with minimal support from adults.

A further consideration, especially with respect to the matter of individuals' privacy is that of the physical placement of computers and their orientation within classrooms. In Cameo 1 the computer screen was visible to the other children in the class and attracted unwanted attention. Had the machine been turned round the interference would have been largely prevented and the children working on it would have had privacy to make their own mistakes, and learn from them without peer comment. Several studies have reported the reluctance of older girls in particular to 'perform in public' on the computer using Logo (Finlayson 1985), word processing or drill and practice programs (Underwood *et al.* 1995). As we noted in Chapter 3, by using relatively private ILS computers, underachieving boys are prepared to work hard and show what they are capable of, without loosing their 'cool' image in class (Brown and Underwood 1997). Younger children, both boys and girls, seem to be less susceptible to such challenges to their self-image, but providing an element of privacy for working remains an important part of managing the overall learning with ICT in every class.

Children acting within contexts

Two dimensions are important in respect of this, as can be seen in Figure 4.1. These are:

1 The social context which is created by the children in their inter-action with the computer and the software. This includes their task talk, problem-solving tactics, turn-taking decisions, negotiations and so on. These will be discussed further in Chapter 5.
2 The curriculum context – that is, the subject area in the National Curriculum in which the IT is experienced.

IT is unique within the National Curriculum in that although it has its own programme of study related to 'IT capability', children are expected to 'develop and apply their IT capability in their study of National Curriculum subjects' (DfE 1995). IT is essentially about processes, but these cannot be learned without content. The value of IT in education lies in the contribution it can make to children's learning in other curriculum subjects, en-hancing and expanding the range of learning opportunities. There is no conflict between learning IT and learning another curriculum subject *through* IT, as the programme of study for IT at Key Stage 1 stresses: 'Pupils should be taught to use IT equipment and software confidently and *purposefully* to communicate and handle information, and to support their problem solving, recording and expressive work' (DfE 1995: 68, emphasis added).

In fact, all ICT learning should take place within other curriculum subjects, and *support good practice* within those subjects. At Key Stage 2 children should also learn to: 'become discerning in their use of IT; select information, sources and media for their suitability for purpose; and assess the value of IT in their working practices' (DfE 1995: 69). If children are to learn to be discerning in their use of IT, then teachers must certainly be so, and software chosen to support the needs of the subjects.

ICT capability is defined as the knowledge and skills which enable children to make effective use of ICT tools in order to:

- analyse;
- process and present information;
- model;
- measure and control external events;
- solve problems.

This list relates to the children's understanding of ICT in the world of work and wider society as well as to the curriculum. The National Curriculum document is written in terms of the processes which are enabled by using ICT, rather than the techniques of using particular programs, as we discussed in Chapter 3. Clearly, planning needs to be carried out to ensure that these requirements are met across all the curriculum subjects, as we discuss in Chapter 6.

Differentiation

From the child's point of view the accurate match of task demand to their ability is critical to maintaining progress both *in* ICT and in learning *through* ICT. High and low attaining children are the ones most often affected by inappropriate levels of task demand. Planning is most often directed to the *average* range of ability with ICT, as with everything else. Carpenter (1995: 215) suggests differentiation as the key feature of effective and inclusive teaching and learning and lists the important elements of this as:

- teaching based on the assessed capability of the learner;
- children working at their own pace;
- provision of alternative activities for individuals;
- opportunities for children to learn in cooperative groups;
- children taking some responsibility for their learning;
- development of children's reflexivity about learning.

ICT seems to present really worthwhile opportunities for making a contribution to this process, especially with one or two class

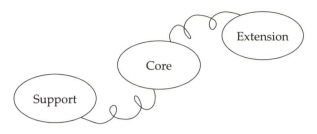

Figure 4.3   Carpenter's differentiation spiral
Source: Carpenter (1995: 219).

computers used by small groups. Even in a multiple machine setting, however, there are ways of allowing children to work at their own rate without getting too far behind, as we saw in Cameo 2. Alternatively, different tasks or a range of different software could be running within a computer lab, to make more demands on the higher attaining children.

Another helpful idea here which Carpenter (1995: 219) offers is the 'differentiation spiral' (see Figure 4.3). The idea is that all children will engage in some dimension of the core activity but low attaining children will have a series of stepped activities leading up to that level, while high achievers would start with the core and then continue to extend their knowledge and skill base. In Cameo 3 the children with special educational needs were able to achieve a great deal because of the extra support provided. Parent-helpers or classroom aides are most useful here, if you are lucky enough to have them, but older children or more experienced peers can also occasionally provide this support. Explaining what you already know and can do, breaking down your knowledge into readily accessible bits, can provide valuable consolidation work for the more experienced peers (see Chapter 5).

Children's contribution to assessment

On a day-to-day basis children should have an active role in recording their own achievement, both because they are active learners and in order to foster their reflexivity. The very youngest children can operate simple pictorial records even if teachers need to add subsequent information about the children's attitudes to

learning and their levels of success within defined learning outcomes. For example, self-recorded computer-printed certificates:

> My name is:
>
> Today's date is:
>
> I can use: (program name)
>
> to (purpose for which it was used)

For computer handling, similar certificates can be printed, and as
they will be done within a simple word processor, they are also
a record of early word-processing work. In the early stages the
child need only type in his or her name in the appropriate place
on the certificate. Later on they can include more details of the
work they have actually done:

> I can load the program
>
> I can save my work
>
> I can print out my work

The certificates can be printed out by the children themselves,
signed and dated by the teacher and taken home to show parents
before being kept in the children's own record of achievement
folder. Such certificates can be particularly motivating for children
who are less successful academically. They can also structure the
skills which children will be expected to achieve each year, so
that when they go into the next class the new teacher will know
what they have achieved and can continue to build on this. As
will be illustrated in Chapter 6, it is crucial that teachers know
what is happening in other classes.

Summary

We have considered the concept of context, examined the teacher's
role as manager of the learning context, and examined children
as active learners within the tasks they are set. There has been a
focus particularly on the physical organization, the choice and
setting up of software, the task organization and the recording
assessment and evaluation of the learning. In the next chapter

we consider the social nature of this learning and how it can be developed within groups of children.

Points to consider

1 Draw a plan of the current arrangement of furniture in your classroom and consider the 'best' arrangement you could achieve if you had one, two or even three computers available. Create a list of the resource materials you would provide to support the pupils work when using two specific programs. What additional resources would be essential for you to work with more than one machine? What additional 'training' would your particular class require to work in this way?
2 What amendments would you need to make to your existing pupil profiles or records to include the identification of ICT developments and progression in the learning of individuals?
3 Imagine you are introducing your pupils to a new program and outline what you would say to them to make it clear exactly *why* they will be working with it. Develop a certificate to show the early relevant skills children might achieve.

5

Supporting learning

Cameo I

Two 9-year-olds, Ruth and Joe, are at the computer writing a story together. Joe is at the keyboard while Ruth sits slightly away to one side, watching the screen. She makes a few suggestions for words to use, but Joe ignores them and continues entering his own ideas.

'Can I have a go then?' asks Ruth after a while.

'Yes, all right!' responds Joe, and moves his chair slightly to one side while pushing the mouse over towards Ruth. He sits looking around at the class while Ruth types in a few words, then turns and comments that she has spelled a word wrong. Ruth presses the delete button and deletes all the words up to the offending one, retypes it and laboriously sets about retyping all the other words.

Cameo 2

Two 7-year-old girls, Nicola and Suki, are working on a My World screen, moving blocks to create sets of different attributes. The whole time they are discussing their moves and making suggestions to each other.

'Oh, put that one there.'

'We could make this a set of yellow ones.'

'Or yellow ones with corners.'

'Shall I put this blue one there?'

'No, you can't do that, put the triangle in.'

'That's not got four corners . . .'

At each move they pass the mouse between them, and both intently watch the screen whether they are operating the mouse or not.

> **Cameo 3**
>
> A Year 6 class are helping set up a butterfly garden on ground next to their school. They have been finding out about plants which attract butterflies and are now using a simple structured database on the computer to discover what food the caterpillars of different butterflies and moths eat. The program has a capability for searching the data, sorting it alphabetically or numerically and graphing on selected fields. In order to help the children familiarize themselves with these different facilities they have been given some questions to address.
>
> June reads out the first of these: 'Which insect has the largest wingspan?'
>
> Greg says, 'That's easy. We want to use "search". Look at all the ones with wingspans bigger than . . .'
>
> Fatima chips in: 'Bigger than what? How big are they anyway?'
>
> 'I don't know. Could we have a look at some records and see the wingspans in those or draw a block-graph?'
>
> The teacher asks, 'How will a block-graph help us?'
>
> 'It will give us a picture of how big they are, and then we can pick the biggest.'
>
> 'We can see how big "big" is.'
>
> 'That is a good idea! Has anyone else any suggestions?' asks the teacher.
>
> 'Wait a minute! Can't we use "sort" instead of "search"?'
>
> 'Yes, if we sort them into order of wingspan. Then we'll get the biggest one first!'
>
> 'Two good ideas!' says the teacher. 'Choose which one to use. I'll come back in a couple of minutes.'

Introduction

Earlier we used the key Vygotskian idea of the ZPD and described how this outlines the difference between the level of activity which children can manage to complete successfully without any help and the more advanced level to which they aspire, and achieve when some assistance is available to them. A metaphor which is frequently associated with the ZPD is that of 'scaffolding' (Wood *et al.* 1976). Scaffolding supports a building in its construction phase so that it will develop according to the designer's plans. When we apply this metaphor to children's learning we must not overlook the fact that, unlike a building, they have an active part in the 'construction process'. This is an important dimension of 'mindful learning'.

Early work exploring the metaphor of scaffolding involved the interactions of very young children and their mothers and these studies recount how the adults gradually help the learners to accomplish tasks too difficult for them to complete alone. This is a very special form of instruction, one in which the actions of the learner and those of the more experienced person are totally interrelated. It is, in fact, a co-construction of thinking, heavily reliant on the sensitivity of the adults' intervention to the learning needs of the child. The link between thinking and this kind of instruction in classroom learning is one which Vygotsky stressed (see Moll and Whitmore 1993), and he emphasized that language manipulation and the communication of meanings are central characteristics of learning. Formal, or more systematic instruction, in Vygotsky's view, was a stage in development which properly followed that of play in the overall development of children.

In their account of the SLANT (Spoken Languages and New Technologies) project Wegerif and Scrimshaw (1997) point out the close connections between the ideas of the ZPD and scaffolding but also add that these concepts lack clarity in terms of 'operational definitions' for use in classrooms. Nevertheless, the scaffolding metaphor is felt to be a useful one and they offer a number of helpful definitions. We take what might be described as a broad view of scaffolding, one which recognizes that some people are very much more effective in this support role than others. For us, *scaffolding* requires that:

- the learner is an active participant – it is not about digesting predetermined chunks of information;
- the 'teacher' sees support as leading the learner towards eventual independent completion of the task;
- talk and other literate behaviours are part of the action;
- the learner is gaining some kind of meaning from within the context of the shared activity even if this is, as yet, incomplete;
- the process will need to change and develop over time as the learner becomes more experienced and competent.

We look first at how group members help each other and at different *agents* who support learning within small group activities at the computer. Some of these examples would readily be recognized as scaffolding – others are less directly so. We also include aspects of the teaching role as examples of scaffolding and consider how displays, prompts and reactions of the computer software which provide the computer context also support the learning.

The child

In each of the cameos children are engaged in joint activities of some kind involving computers. In Cameo 1, Ruth and Joe find themselves in a situation which is not at all uncommon in classrooms, although in working together on the construction of a joint narrative, the type of discussion between this pair remains very much at the level of which key to press rather than that of developing and sharing ideas about what could happen in their story. Each of them is taking a turn to input some information and each is contributing some suggestions. Involvement remains, however, at a minimal level of *cooperation*. In this cameo the computer simply displays for them the results of their efforts: the full range of tools which word processing offers them as authors is not being used.

The girls depicted in Cameo 2 are engaged in a more *collaborative* effort. They see the task set by the teacher as a joint enterprise which depends on each of them making efforts to produce the best outcome they can between them. As they work they share something of their inner thinking. Their talk is not in itself complete: to understand what is going on in their joint activity the listener needs to be able to see the screen display which the children can see. This common visual focus is essential to their efforts to make sense of the set-building task on which they are working. Talk and the common field of reference provided by the computer are critical to the learning. One main feature which distinguishes collaboration from cooperation is the shared ownership of the outcome, which may be better than either of the girls in Cameo 2 would have produced on her own. (See Crook 1994 for detailed discussion of cooperative and collaborative working.)

The larger group in Cameo 3 are working collaboratively in a number of different ways. They share the overall class objective to complete the project establishing the butterfly sanctuary and, as an aspect of this, are finding out which plants are essential if the caterpillars are to develop as they should. At the same time they are learning to use the database facilities effectively, and helping each other in their understanding through discussion. The questions turn the group activity into a problem-solving task, where they not only have to find solutions, but find each one in an efficient way making best use of the facilities. The challenges to each other's ideas and suggestions may sound a little argumentative, but comments are kept at a friendly level and provoke the children into justifying or explaining their viewpoints.

The teacher in Cameo 3 was able to use a commercially available data file with reliable information on butterflies and moths to help with the project and alongside this set a few questions to illustrate how the three facilities of *'search'*, *'sort'* and *'graph'* could be used. (See the appendix for details about structured databases.)

Grouping children

Choosing children to work together in small groups at the computer is a far from simple process, but when the resulting groups work collaboratively, the evidence shows that this is beneficial to their individual learning (Light 1993). Collaboration is also important for the children's social development and results in a more pleasant working atmosphere in the classroom.

Successful group work is achieved when this approach is familiar to the children. Plenty of practical experiences of working in this way should be given over time in order to achieve success. First thoughts about Ruth and Joe's interaction might suggest that it was not an entirely happy experience for them. In our second cameo the girls seem to be very comfortable in their collaboration. They demonstrate in their action and talk that in this classroom it is definitely acceptable to help each other and that what the teacher is expecting is one piece of work as a result of their joint efforts. The slightly larger group of boys and girls using the database in Cameo 3 don't seem at all inhibited by working with each other. Gender seems of lesser importance to them than to Ruth and Joe, and they know that sharing ideas and explanations between them is an important aspect of their task.

Research suggests that girls in our society more naturally behave in a collaborative way at the computer than boy/boy or boy/girl pairs (Hoyles 1988). Girls seem to prefer collaborative situations and when engaged in using word processors or in problem-solving tasks, girl/girl pairs are more likely than others to discuss their approaches and come to joint decisions (Underwood *et al.* 1990).

Boys often choose to work on their own, rather than as a pair, and when put together have a tendency to compete rather than collaborate. However this behaviour is strongly dependent on the classroom climate set by the school and teacher's expectations (Dawes 1997). We worked in two classrooms with single gender pairs of 7-year-olds, observing and tape recording their work at the computer. They had all clearly been taught to cooperate and share the mouse in computer tasks. However several pairs of boys, though not all of them, effectively and subversively obstructed each other's efforts to add text to a jointly agreed screen picture. Like Nicola and Suki these boys had arranged objects on a screen, and were then writing sentences as explanation. Both boys and girls were scrupulously fair in taking turns using the mouse to produce the joint display, though the language of the boys was more disputative, e.g. 'I bet you can't do . . .'; 'Mine's better than yours', whereas the girls only gave supportive comments, e.g. 'That *is* good'; 'I like that idea'.

When it came to sentence writing the girls remained supportive and assisted each other verbally. The boys, on the other hand, clearly thought the rules of behaviour were different. They positioned themselves at either end of the keyboard, so that the one who was typing in the sentence had the 'assistance' of the other pressing SHIFT, RETURN and DELETE in the middle of their typing efforts. The typist tried to defend his work by putting an arm round the keyboard, but nevertheless took several attempts to finish the task (Finlayson and Cook 1998). The class teacher was most certainly unaware of this type of behaviour, and the boys involved took care not to alert her attention.

Underwood (1998: 38) found that it is 'only when boys and girls are paired together that they perform poorly'. However, each child's view may change when they have a specific task and partner in mind. When one is unsure about the viability of a potential pair or group working collaboratively together, careful observation and monitoring help to establish that the desired teacher outcome is achievable in terms of the group interactions.

The question of group size is much less complex, at least when we are thinking about computer-based activities. The key question must be how many children can realistically see the standard-sized screen comfortably. The answer: two, or a *maximum* of three. With groups of this size it is important to ensure that each child is clear about how the work is to be shared. Whoever operates the input device (e.g. the mouse) controls the activity. If the desired behaviour is strict rotation of turns then that is what the children need to know. Equally they need to know if one partner is to help the other when a difficult point is reached: this is a situation more akin to peer tutoring than group work, an approach found successful in the Bristol Education On-Line Project (Davis 1998).

The role of peers in supporting learning

Our cameos show that different kinds of shared activity can produce different types of interaction, both with the computer and between the individuals involved. More successful collaborations show children securing a greater degree of engagement with the task and a clearer understanding of the aims. Children need to take each other seriously, as meaning-makers. There must be a certain degree of trust between them and a valuing of the others' contribution: respectful and reasoned rejection is acceptable. Equally, the children need to know that their attempts to make meaning jointly are valued by the important adults around them. Scaffolding is often considered in respect of interactions between the less and more experienced partners but, in the cameos the participants are members of the same peer group. Given our broad definition of scaffolding processes we are happy to extend the idea to include children supporting the learning of their peers.

Forman and McPhail (1993: 260) found that children are able to support each other to 'establish, modify, reflect on and refine their initial task goals and definitions in order to collaborate'. Hence, *mediation* may offer a more appropriate metaphor than *scaffolding*. It is the social interactions *mediated by talk* which cause changes in learning. Vygotsky felt that meaning-making activity, especially involving language and the use of multiple sign systems (including literate behaviours of all kinds), allowed the child to 'appropriate' new knowledge. Learning can therefore be seen as mediated through:

- the teacher;
- language as a psychological tool;
- the computer as a cultural tool.

Looked at in this way, we believe that it is through, and within, their group work discussions at the computer that children, operating as a peer group, may mediate each other's learning processes. The teacher's planning, preparation and careful selection of software also help mediation to occur.

The role of talk at the computer

The talk between Ruth and Joe in Cameo 1 is very limited in its scope and rather more related to the low level mechanics of using the program than to an 'on task' discussion involving them in engaging with its intellectual demands. Farish (1989) considers this latter dimension to be essential for collaborative learning. The principal dimensions of the Spoken Language and New Technology (SLANT) project were those of talk and technology within a socio-cultural view of learning and Wegerif and Scrimshaw (1997) offer teachers a most valuable source of information and discussion as well as very detailed analyses of all these dimensions. One of a number of very helpful suggestions for considering analytically the quality of children's talk exchanges is offered by Fisher (1997: 35) who outlines three broad categories of talk to be commonly found in the project classroom. These she defines as:

1 *Disputative*: initiating (proposal, hypothesis or instruction) followed by disagreement and contradiction without reason.
2 *Cumulative*: initiating followed by agreement without discussion or development – participants echo suggestions or agree with one another without question.
3 *Exploratory*: initiation challenged and counter-challenged, but hypotheses are developed and supported by giving reasons for dissent. Exploratory talk can be characterized by words such as *why; because; if . . . so; might; could; would; should; think; maybe* which indicate that pupils are offering ideas for consideration and reflecting on those offered by their peers in a manner which indicates decision making based on some supporting argument or evidence.

Fisher suggests that exploratory talk indicates that pupils are extending their learning within their ZPD as participants are 'playing an important role to enable learning which goes beyond itself' (Fisher 1997: 36).

The context

Chapter 4 considered *context, setting,* and *environment* and the links between them. The term *environment* relates to the general ambience of classrooms which affects the children's understanding of what behaviour is allowed. For group work to be successful children need to understand that helping each other is an important part of the learning task, not something to be shunned as 'cheating'. They also need to know how to disagree with each other with respect and politeness, and how to value each other's contribution to the group.

The context level relates to those aspects of learning which we have described as social and curriculum contexts. Some mention of social context – the way groups support each other – has been made in our consideration of the child's perspective. But how does the curriculum context affect learner support in ICT?

Software which encourages collaborative work and discussion is the primary focus of this section rather than that relating to specific subject domains, though all examples would also have subject dimensions, such as geographical understanding or mathematical reasoning.

Wegerif and Scrimshaw (1997) explored the type of computer tasks most likely to promote useful discussion between small groups of children. They consider that adventure games offer rich opportunities for developing collaborative, group and problem-solving situations. This view is also supported by a number of other studies such as Crook (1987) and Whitebread (1997). In addition, Logo programming, although located in a more specifically mathematical context, is felt to provide similar experiences (Hoyles and Sutherland 1989).

Although adventure games can present a range of differently challenging tasks, some require a more thoughtful approach by the teacher than others. Phillips and Scrimshaw (1997) suggest that adventures with intrinsic problems to solve – that is, where the problem is an integral part of the overall story context – lead to better discussions than those with 'inserted', unrelated problems. Whitebread (1997) claims that children do much better when the adventure presents them with meaningful contexts where they can use knowledge of the 'real world' to help solve the problems and so develop logic. The problems presented need to have some open-endedness about them, so that different moves made by the children will lead to different outcomes.

Some 'too simple' adventure programs have only one 'right route' to a solution which can be found by trial and error, tempting children to go for quick answers. Such programs have less learning potential for children. It is important that children hypothesize about possible outcomes in adventure games because it is this process and the ensuing discussions which extends their current understandings and draws upon outside knowledge. This development of children's reasoning abilities makes good adventure games valuable learning experiences.

In turtle graphics and Logo programing teachers may specify a particular end point to children without restricting the range of approaches available for completing the task. The computer program actively contributes to the learning situation by presenting visual evidence for the group to consider. Computers have a role to play in encouraging learners to help each other to understand and collaborate in order to solve their problems.

In both Adventure games and Logo the computer plays an active role in responding to the decisions of the users. Similarly, Cameo 3 shows a computer database in a powerful role, sorting, searching and displaying information in accordance with the commands entered. With spreadsheets and databases the computer is taking an active part in promoting interaction between learners. It is an active partner in the children's learning, giving them important feedback which encourages them to review their decisions. Such *active* uses of the computer provide assistance to children in problem solving and so have a 'mediating' role in the learning process. The software acts as a 'dialogic partner'.

In the first two cameos, on the other hand, the computer has a more *passive* role, providing a shared display screen on which the writing and the sets are presented. In each task, the keyboard and mouse exist as shared input devices through which the children can communicate with the computer. In neither case does the computer give any evaluative feedback, positive suggestions or options for the children's response but merely reflects their own ideas back to them. Even in such a passive mode the computer offers positive support to learners because the screen display acts as a focal medium through which children can explore their own and each other's thinking. They can read back their story, check it for continuity and flow, see if their created sets are consistent or contradictory and then refine their ideas – for example, from 'corners' to 'square corners'.

Much educational software come into this category of passive applications but does not necessarily produce collaborative work. To maximize software potential other factors are important. The teacher's actions are critical in setting up learning tasks before the children take part in them, and subsequently in monitoring and intervening when children are working with them. (Finlayson and Cook 1998 discuss active and passive software more fully.)

The teacher

In many classroom settings it is not always possible for teachers to devote extensive periods of time to working with individuals. In our discussion we have indicated how we see other children, the computer and its software as also having some part in supporting learning. In Chapter 6 we will show how national and local policies and other outside school issues have an impact on whole school decision making and on what it is possible for individual teachers to offer in their own classrooms. Many decisions have to be taken at the school level before teachers can engage in detailed consideration of the ways in which they can offer learning support in ICT tasks to school-aged children.

The idea of 'pre'-scaffolding

A useful way of thinking about the teacher's role within class activities is to consider decisions made *before* the children are involved in ICT work. We could say that advanced decisions are offering support as 'pre'-scaffolding for children's learning experiences. Many are issues of general classroom management where the teacher decides:

- why and for whom the work is most appropriate at a particular moment in time;
- which children will best work together for a specific purpose;
- where the ICT activity will take place (laptops, computer room or classroom);
- what the learning targets will be for each particular application.

Decisions about how software supports the learning activity in terms of ICT capability and curriculum dimension are also part of the teacher's pre-scaffolding actions. Perhaps the most important of all is 'hooking them into learning', capitalizing on what we know about children's motivation and enthusiasm in working with all sorts of technology, especially computers.

Intervention: assisting actual performance

When children are working with computers the teacher has to be involved in the activity – at least intermittently – so that she or he can monitor events as they develop and take advantage of opportunities for intervention. Being able to take advantage of these moments can be somewhat opportunistic. As they spend time with each group in turn, teachers will be able to provide feedback, ask children questions which challenge the level of their thinking, or encourage them to be more explicit in their verbal communication. Equally, teachers will make observations which will allow them to evaluate the children's performance.

As well as opportunistic interventions, some can be planned. For example, teachers can build in 'pupil report' moments, where children give an account of work in progress before they leave the computer. Alternatively, 'pupil reports' can be given by several groups to the class on completion of computer work, almost as a plenary session. This more formal approach allows the teacher to:

- probe further into children's activities;
- assist pupils in developing their abilities in preparing and delivering verbal reports;
- highlight successful strategies developed by one group which would be of help to the others;
- get the class to work together on unresolved problems.

This type of work may actually require pupil training.

In our broad definition of scaffolding we included the idea that supporting learning is an active and dynamic process. Teachers need to have a clear view of learning goals and recognize that their role is that of supporting the learners in such a way as to allow them gradually to do more and more for themselves. This is true for the very youngest as well as the very oldest learners, so clearly the amount of assistance offered, and the way in which support is given, will vary from child to child, across time and in relation to the difficulty and novelty of the task. In Chapter 3 we used the term 'assisted performance' to describe this process. The term was devised by Tharpe (1993) who puts forward a model of teaching behaviour which he feels is responsive and flexible. By this he means that interactions in classrooms need to:

- begin with the child's current level of understanding;
- consequently allow the child a meaningful role in the setting of the instructional task or goal;
- include helping behaviours by the teacher that assist the student to pursue these goals and move from one level to the next; by
- pulling performance from the child, so a productive communication or creation by the child is the vehicle for instantiating new knowledge (Tharpe 1993: 272).

Tharpe (1993: 272) outlines seven strategies which can be used by teachers to assist performance so that an *instructional conversation* can be established. The most effective of all his strategies is, he says, that of providing *feedback*. This allows the learner to judge how close his or her effort is to the target to be achieved. The other six strategies are:

- *Modelling*: allowing the child to observe the way an experienced person accomplishes a task.
- *Contingency management:* the teacher makes use of rewards and sanctions so that the learner is supported in completing the task.
- *Instructing*: especially useful when the learner cannot quite manage everything alone, and the teacher provides information or asks for a particular response so that the learner can make decisions which help them move forward.
- *Questioning*: the teacher tries to help the learner think through ideas to make a talk response which is more significant than could have been made without the 'probe'.
- *Cognitive structuring*: the teacher offers a structure or explanation which helps the learner make sense of their new learning.
- *Task structuring:* the teacher organizes the task so that learners, with this support, are able to operate in the ZPD when, without this help, the task would be too much for them.

Table 5.1 shows how Tharpe's seven strategies might be related specifically to ICT work.

Table 5.1   Examples of Tharpe's (1993) strategies for assisting performance, adapted for ICT

Strategy	Teacher	Computer software	Peer group
Modelling	Through whole-class demonstrations of software, offers a model of the process	Can take a pupil step by step through a procedure	Children often model for each other particular techniques or moves in problem-solving tasks
Feedback	Indicates to pupils the acceptability of their problem-solving approach and procedural steps	Offers information to the learner which allows for self correction	Children guide the thinking of others by their comments, suggestions, corrections
Contingency management	Celebrates success as part of pupil reporting phase to encourage a desired behaviour in others	Success with tasks or the application of specific tasks or problems solved is highly motivating	Peer pressure influences the behaviour of group members
Instructing	Part of the teacher's introduction and task setting	Often, programs re-offer problems in a different way or request learners to carry out specific activities	Children direct others as a result of their own experiences
Questioning	Requires from the learner a verbal response which comes about as a result of more sophisticated thinking	Programs contain specific problems which must be solved before moving on to the next phase	Pupils challenge each other by their questions about actions, techniques or world knowledge

Table 5.1 cont'd

Strategy	Teacher	Computer software	Peer group
Cognitive structuring	Part of the teacher's task-setting decision making, making goals clear, explaining procedures	Provides clues, offers suggestions, uses formats known to the pupils	Peer tutoring activities, when one pupil gives hints to others
Task structuring	Helping learners to work through component parts of the task so that they are actively working in the ZPD	Breaking down a task into component parts and re-presenting these as a series of manageable steps	Help with suggestions about actions drawn from their own experiences

Some of Tharpe's strategies can be seen in Cameo 3. The teacher gives positive feedback which rewards the children for their efforts so far. She asks questions which require the children to be more explicit in their talk, and probes for other possible solutions or strategies to use. Finally, she asks them to make a decision which, in this case, is helping to structure the task for the group by encouraging them to move into the next stage in the overall process.

What is important for ICT learning is the 'joint activity' – that is, the way the learners and the learning support mechanisms of teacher, computer program and fellow group members work together so that the highest possible level of performance becomes achievable. Such a successful coming together of elements may necessitate some preparatory activities.

Training for working together

Teachers may decide to train a class in cooperative and collaborative behaviours to encourage them to become autonomous learners. Although adventure games are very good for encouraging group interaction and constructive talk, teachers are not always satisfied with the natural performance of their pupils.

Dawes (1997) was disappointed with the level of discussion which was evident when children in her class first began to work with these programs. She decided that to improve the situation she needed to 'teach them about talk'. She began working, off the computer, in whole-class and small groups on a variety of listening and talking tasks. One of the early problems was that of one individual allocating blame for failure or claiming credit for success when working in a small group. After a term of 'talking lessons' the children discussed and agreed on ground rules for effective talk at the computer:

- No one in the group could claim credit for successful ideas, and no one could be held solely responsible for errors.
- Each member of the group must be asked for their ideas by the others. Everyone's ideas must be given equal consideration.
- When a group member suggests an idea, they must be asked to give a reason for it, and given time to state the reason.
- The group must have agreed on anything entered into the computer.
- Decisions about who will be the 'typist', who makes written notes if required, and so on, must be sorted out before work begins on the computer.
- If things become difficult or disheartening, the entire group must seek assistance from the teacher or one of their classmates. No one individual can opt out from the activity.

(Dawes 1997: 194)

A very useful source of ideas for practical activities which develop children's awareness of talk is the National Oracy Project publication (Baddeley, undated, circa 1992). This gives details about information seeking and sharing (jigsaw techniques), checking information sources (envoying) and clarifying understanding by working in a 'triad' which has inbuilt talker, questioner and recording roles.

Assessing aspects of group work

A central idea in this chapter is that of the ZPD. When we want to make assessments of children working in this pedagogical space we as teachers need to be actively involved in the learning interactions. In this way it is possible to make informed judgements about the ways in which learners respond to hints, suggestions, instructions, questions and feedback. This allows us to make 'dynamic assessments' of learning capacity rather than just arriving at a judgement of what learners already know. Such assessments could be recorded as brief action notes and included in pupils' overall records. Positive signs of development would be an increased willingness on the part of children to take greater responsibility for their own learning, as well as a readiness to become involved in trying things out or risk taking.

As this chapter has also shown, talk is another critical dimension. In fact the SLANT project claims that 'language is the essential medium of learning' (Wegerif and Scrimshaw 1997: 3). No assessment would be complete without some acknowledgement of the ways in which children use this medium to promote learning.

When ICT is a main component of the learning task, teachers will also want to evaluate the contribution of the software itself and its associated support materials. The potential utility of the software for the age group and curriculum area will have been evaluated by the ICT coordinator and school staff at the time of its purchase, but this further evaluation goes beyond the initial point to consider the way the application works out in actual classroom practice. For instance, Cameo 1 suggests that the word processor was not being used to its best advantage. The children needed to know more about working as a pair in the process of collaborative writing. In contrast, Cameo 3 indicates that the database program operates at a suitable level for the pupils and makes a considerable contribution to their developing understanding because they have a very clear view of the target set.

Summary

This chapter has considered support for learners working with computers from: their peer group with whom they share tasks; the computer and its software, which is supplying and supporting the task; and the teacher. Pupils can mediate each other's learning and, through collaborative work, achieve more than they would alone. The computer software and teacher together can provide and make use of a supportive framework for children's

ICT use. The teacher is in a position to provide opportunistic scaffolding for the children when observing and recognizing teachable moments in computer tasks. The teacher also has responsibility for assessing the quality of learning taking place.

Points to consider

1 Collect talk samples from small groups working at the computer and use a simple coding system to ask and answer questions about what the talk tells us about how children are learning. Fisher's (1997) categories could be used, or the categories shown in Table 5.2.
2 Devise a sheet for children to use to record their own ideas on 'How I worked as a group member'.
3 As a staff group exercise collect brief observational video samples of about five minutes each showing children throughout the school talking in twos or threes using similar types of software. Look for evidence of increasing skill in speaking and listening, and in using the software. If the children are in same/ mixed gender groups, are they all taking a full part in the work?

Further reading

For those who wish to read more about how successful small group work can be established in the classroom, Reid *et al.* (1989), Forrestal (1992) and Dunne and Bennett (1990) are all strongly recommended.

Table 5.2 Children's use of talk in collaborative learning

What are they doing?	How are they learning?	What are they learning?
Sharing ideas	Reordering what they know	To understand information
Sorting ideas		To elicit information
Justifying points of view	Applying what they know to a new situation	To make explicit their thinking and the thinking of others
Summarizing	Making connections	To share attitudes and feelings supportively
Supporting with evidence		To explore and command the language of learning
Reordering		
Questioning		
Speculating		
Offering reasons		
Arguing		
Building on ideas		
Getting information		
Seeking clarification		
Hypothesizing		
Exploring cause and effect		
Refining observations, language and thinking		
Reviewing		

Source: Baddeley (undated, circa 1992: 41).

6

Whole school issues

Cameo 1

A Year 5 class have all been investigating the properties of
metals and non-metals, carrying out a number of tests on small
samples of materials such as wood, candle wax, aluminium foil
and copper sheeting. Two computers have been set up with
word processors using on-screen word banks. These allow
text, whole words or phrases, shown on a grid at the bottom
of the screen, to be entered with a mouse click.

One group of three pupils come to one of the computers to
write up their science experiment. They use mainly the words
and phrases in the word bank to record their findings:
'Aluminium will bend. It is shiny. The bulb lit up, so it will
conduct electricity. It is not magnetic.' A second group use the
other computer. This is a more able group and they have a
different word bank set up containing only the key scientific
words related to their experiments. They write their report
using both the normal keyboard and these words, as they are
required.

In the same science class one boy, Edward, is working on the
experiments with two others, but has his own computer on
which the results are being entered. Edward is partially sighted,
so his screen is set up with a particular coloured background
and large black letters which he is able to read. He cannot
distinguish the words on the word bank but uses the right
mouse button to get the computer to read each one out before
deciding whether to use it. When they have finished Edward
gets the word processor to read out the whole text to check
it, and they all laugh at the mispronunciation of aluminium.

Cameo 2

First thing in the morning Ms Berry is checking-in the portable computers which pupils have borrowed overnight, making sure that the batteries are put on charge and helping the children to print out their finished work. She is standing in a corner of the inner hall next to a storage cupboard. The laptops are kept in numbered slots in the cupboard when they are not being used. Next to the cupboard is a table on which there are two printers with leads to which the computers can be connected, for printing out, and further along are the battery charging connections.

Three monitors from Class 3 arrive. 'Mrs Carlton says please can we have six machines for our history – we are going out on a field trip!' These are signed out to them. A Year 6 boy comes to borrow a machine to finish off his design project. Ms Berry tells him: 'You must bring it back by break because Mr Lynford's class have booked them all for the rest of the morning.'

Cameo 3

The headteacher and ICT coordinator are discussing the possible purchase of a new piece of software.

'If we get this new spreadsheet who is going to use it?'

All the Year 5 and Year 6 classes. They should be investigating mathematical patterns and working out science results and things like that on it.'

'Yes, but who can use the software?'

'Well I should think a lot of the staff have used spreadsheets for their own record keeping and budgets and things – I know the history and science coordinators regularly do their equipment orders on them, but we will need to run some training sessions for some of the others.'

'Is this spreadsheet the same as the ones they've used before?'

'Well all spreadsheets are pretty similar, but there may be one or two quirks about this one. I haven't used it myself yet.'

'Will we need to send people on external courses then?'

'Oh I shouldn't think so. I could do an introductory demonstration – you know, this is the program, this is what you can do with it, and these are the sort of applications we want to use it for. Then the staff can have a play with it, and I'll see how many want proper sessions to develop the teaching work.'

Introduction

In Chapter 4 we mentioned that a range of outside forces have an influential role in affecting what actually happens in classrooms. Teachers work within a number of constraints in their curriculum decision making: school, local and national policies are examples. The interactions between teachers and children have always been, and will always remain, the central concern of education, but these are influenced by many things. While the dimensions of these may change, the *quality* of children's learning rests very much on the quality of teacher-pupil interactional exchanges (Woods and Jeffrey 1996). Sociocultural views of learning recognize that the goals and purposes of schooling are influenced strongly by each society's view of the purposes of education. From this stance what happens in individual classrooms at the micro level is the outcome of a series of actions and counter-actions occurring between events and ideas generated at the national (or macro level) and implemented within specific schools. This is part of the normal process of change. Sometimes the rate of change can feel uncomfortable, but no one would expect something as dynamic and exciting as educating the next generation to be an unchanging process. This chapter considers issues relating to the role of technology within this overall process of development addressed at whole school level: a level positioned between the micro and macro tiers identified above.

Throughout this book we have emphasized the positive advantages of using computers within the framework of established and proven good practice. The energy created by children purposefully engaged with challenging tasks is a powerful force for learning and we want to make sure that their overall experience has an integrity which will emerge from a coherent whole school programme.

A clear ICT policy is of prime importance in setting out the school's intentions and identifying ways in which an integral technological experience will be provided for children as they progress through the school. Provision of machines and software, and developments in the use of both across the age and ability range, are seen as central dimensions of a whole school policy. Ways of helping to ensure a child's progression through increasing challenges, and the achievement of an overall balance in the cross-curricular use of a range of ICT techniques and processes in the subject areas, are important dimensions.

The child

It is possible to consider whole school issues and the child in two ways. First from the child's point of view and second from the perspective of the adults involved in the immediate school system – the head, class teachers, the governing body and the parents. Essentially all the adults have the children's interests at heart: the child is, after all, the ultimate concern of all these people.

Children have a highly developed sense of 'fairness' and perhaps this might make a useful starting point for examining whole school issues, especially if the word 'equity' is substituted for fairness. The idea underlying this shift is that being fair may not just require an even-handed approach to the provision of ICT experiences in the classroom but, in fact, require rather more. Curriculum differentiation, software selection and classroom management strategies are vital, as is offering access to equipment, which on the surface looks very far from fair. In every dimension of equal opportunity children have a right to 'equity'. In the case of ICT this means that they must be provided with the means to develop their ICT capability in all the domains of knowledge to the maximum level possible. (For further discussion of equity issues, see Downes 1998.)

In Cameo 1 all the children in the class are writing reports about science experiments. Some children need support with reading and writing tasks, and find typing in work from the keyboard slow, laborious and unsatisfying. In our scenario they have been offered varying levels of help with the task; some of them are writing out entire reports from whole words and phrases pre-selected by the teacher and presented in the form of an on-screen word bank. The more able children could have managed with just the normal qwerty keyboard, but get assistance with particular scientific terms and new words they have encountered in their experimental work. This enables them to complete their written work more efficiently than otherwise. This kind of support from time to time means that these children can move on to further scientific explorations in the dedicated lesson time, leaving drafting and editing tasks to be developed on another occasion. Using word banks for all the children makes the tasks appear similar for each of them, but the way in which the words are set up allows for differentiation in the level of support provided. A word bank offering all the required vocabulary and simply structured sentences for less able pupils allows them to achieve a report structure without too much difficulty, providing they are directed to look for key sequencing terms. Edward, the visually impaired child, is able to take a full part in carrying out the science tests. He can read the report which his group is producing as he has the developing text displayed on his special screen.

The children's learning is assisted by the technology in several ways:

- all groups are producing a quick, clear report of the tests they carried out through the use of the word banks;
- by using differentiated word banks, task demands – in terms of difficulty – have been made to suit the ability of the pupils;
- the visually impaired child can take a full part in the activity of his group by having his personal equipment (enhanced screen and speech facility) linked to that being used by his peers.

Word banks and concept keyboards were originally designed to simplify the task of entering information into the computer for children with problems relating to manual dexterity or language impairment. For such children composing and creating written text directly from the standard keyboard, or by hand, presents a considerable barrier to learning. Children who are physically or sensorily challenged can often gain a more equitable access to the entitlement curriculum through the use of technology as exemplified in Cameo 1. Technological support can empower these pupils by allowing them to take a full part in the learning activities of the rest of the class. This point was highlighted in the government white paper *Excellence in Schools* (DfEE 1997) and the NCET publications *Access to Words and Images* (1993) and *Differentiation: Taking IT Forward* (1995). These papers discuss some common adaptations to equipment which can be used to meet children's different needs. Light pens and touch screens are useful but tend to work with very limited software and are expensive. Concept keyboards are now rarely used with mouse-driven computers, but nevertheless selective use of carefully differentiated overlays still has many valuable applications for children with special educational needs (Higgins 1995). This is especially true where teachers are able to add pictures, textures and colours to overlays to emphasize the meaningfulness of tasks for the children. Such features can easily be incorporated onto the overlay sheets covering the touch sensitive pad of the concept keyboard.

Children's needs

While access to computer tasks for some children can be supported by on-screen word banks, concept keyboards or other input devices such as special switches, others will *only* be able to access the curriculum by using a computer, possibly with special adaptations. Children like Edward may be allocated their own computers as literacy aids for use during school time. Schools can offer other children support by allowing additional time to work on computers when fellow class members are using paper and pencil. Equity is conceived of as relating to the needs of children in accessing the curriculum by every appropriate means. Differentiated approaches, such as those already outlined or the use of less complex, or specially designed, software might also be appropriate.

Gifted children and those developing as bilinguals will have needs of a different kind. Such pupils should have opportunities which allow them to develop and to extend their learning in ways which match their strengths and offer them further challenges. Computers can make valuable contributions by, for example, offering word-processing facilities in a range of mother tongues. Covers can be obtained for putting over the QWERTY keys on a normal keyboard. These are sometimes used with very young children to show only lower case letters on the keyboard, rather than the usual upper case ones, but can also be used to display different lettering systems used in Asian languages. Planning individual programmes for very able pupils can be greatly facilitated by using demanding software or more complex tasks. The motivation provided by computer work also helps children to enjoy their education and increases their ability to concentrate and persevere with learning tasks, as well as developing their self-esteem (Cox 1997).

Access and opportunity

Equity for children to develop ICT capability lies in their ability to access computers, and also in their opportunities to do so. This seems particularly difficult to achieve when there are limited resources in school and a very variable level of provision at home. Currently, children come to school with a wide range of different home experiences (Sanger 1997; Downes 1998). These include:

- different language and cultural experiences;
- different social and spatial environments;
- different educational assumptions and expectations.

Whatever their background, children are entitled to develop their ICT competence and to access the richest sources of information available. In order to try to address this problem of differential home access and limited availability in classrooms some schools have acquired as many low-cost computers as possible from every available source. This results in a range of resources being offered to children and staff. While this invariably eases the problem of access, the variety which results from this eclectic approach can put pressure on everyone because of the need to know and understand incompatibilities, especially with older or non-educational machines. However, dedicating different types of machine to specific purposes can minimize these transitional difficulties.

Small palmtops or notepads are usually much cheaper than desktop computers and normally have several educational applications built in – for example, a calculator, a spreadsheet, a graph-drawing tool, a word processor. Children can use the first three tools in their mathematics and science lessons, as appropriate, and use the word processor within many other subject areas. Such tools may not have the sophistication of their desktop counterparts – having limited spellchecking facilities and small screens, for instance – but can offer children the choice of when and where to use them, including on fields trips or for homework tasks.

A stock of such laptop and palmtop computers allows children to access ICT whenever it is appropriate for their learning, overcoming the need to move to a special computer room or to share a few computers in the classroom among 30 pupils. Cameo 2 shows a school taking this approach. Children are allowed to take computers home, and this builds up home-school links as well as enabling the children to continue the work they have begun at school. There is however a cost in terms of organization and time in checking machines in and out, as Ms Berry is doing. However, for schools lucky enough to have a technician this should present no problems. Such usage also helps to overcome the problem of different home provision and can be enormously helpful in allowing parents to understand their child's school activities (Chadwick 1995).

ICT can make a very valuable contribution to strengthening community links as a number of ventures have shown. At Orgill school, which is situated in a high unemployment area of Cumbria, parents are encouraged to come into school to help with computer classes, and evening classes are run to train local adults in ICT skills. This benefits the school and its pupils directly by providing a very knowledgeable and ICT-aware school community and also enhances the work prospects and self-esteem of the adult community. The school is acting as a resource for the entire community and the children are able to develop their own ICT capability with greater understanding and support from home (Lynch 1998).

Children's experience of ICT throughout the school

Children's ICT competence is seen as something which develops throughout their school careers. The rate of technological change means that they will be using entirely different systems at the end of their school life to those available when they were just beginning. After all, as everyone no doubt senses, 'In IT terms tomorrow usually arrives this afternoon' (Tagg 1995: 6). Children need to maintain their rate of progress in order to keep up with the technology and the techniques and skills required to operate it. They need to increase the range of software applications they can use and to develop, from their repeated experiences of similar software applications, new depths of understanding as well as new techniques. One of the strengths of the National Curriculum is that it prevents children who change schools from replicating learning experiences. This problem, however, may still occur in ICT where the technical content has been rather less specifically defined. In the case of ICT children could experience unprofitable repeats of experience if central planning for programmes of study has not been carefully developed. Without whole school planning children could be doing very similar word processing or database work in different classes in the same school! Careful and detailed considerations about the contexts of learning therefore become critical. (This is discussed in detail in the section 'ICT development plan', later in this chapter.)

The context

The context in which children develop their ICT capability is, as discussed in Chapter 4, a multi-layered affair involving:

- the environment (the community in which the school is situated and the ethos developed by the school and in the classroom);
- the setting (the physical resources and layout of computers for learning, and the time constraints);
- the context (the curriculum, software and social elements in which each child works).

Other chapters in this book have focused on the curriculum and social contexts of the children's experiences in school. This chapter is mainly concerned with the environment in which children actually work. It focuses on the school within its community, principally whole school decision making and planning, which need to take place to ensure that pupils gain their ICT entitlement.

The real ICT experience of children in their individual classrooms is determined, to a large extent, by this whole school decision making and planning process as it relates to ICT. The school ICT policy is a crucial document here because it has a key role in setting out specific:

- aims and priorities for ICT;
- responsibilities;
- timescales and budgets;
- monitoring systems.

A school's ICT policy should also link with policies for special educational needs and equal opportunities. All schools are now required to have an ICT development plan, which is an important element of the school development plan.

Each school will, as part of its overall strategy for coping with change in a controlled way, have formulated a school development plan. This is not a document to be perused by interested outsiders but an act of collaboration by the teaching community of the school which identifies and builds on existing strengths. At the same time it indicates how less successful elements will be enhanced over a period of time. The overall purpose of the development plan and its associated documentation is that of school improvement. Within the plan the school will have made clear what are its aims for ICT. The way such plans need to evolve is neatly conceptualized by Tagg (1995: 1):

> Any organisation which cannot find the resources to look to its own strategic development is on the way to terminal decline. Planning and implementing change is a continuous

process. To advance properly, the school development plan must be something which is thought about each week, which produces change – in structure, curriculum, its delivery, its finances – each month and which is reviewed in detail each year.

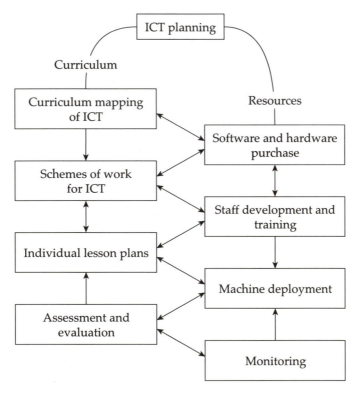

Figure 6.1   Factors involved in ICT planning

ICT development plan

The way in which ICT policy and the ICT development plan relate to other whole school planning issues is shown in Figure 6.1. The various layers depicted all need to have been thought out and be in place to ensure that children achieve their full ICT entitlement. Each level feeds back to the previous one, and all impinge on the ICT development plan.

A detailed school ICT audit makes a sound starting point for the ICT development plan and for the related staff development plan. The audit would be concerned with what software is actually being used, what ICT skills the staff each have, and what software, hardware and relevant curriculum materials are available, so that the desirable state can be mapped onto the existing state and development needs prioritized.

The ICT development plan deals with two main elements: *curriculum management* (the features of which are identified on the left-hand side of Figure 6.1) and *resources management* (whose features are listed on the right-hand side). We have included staff development and training as the teaching staff are undoubtedly the school's most valuable resource.

These two elements interrelate, because the deployment of computers, printers and other peripherals and the way the software and other teaching resources are managed both underpin the detailed planning for ICT which is needed to support the programmes of study throughout each year in each curriculum area.

The planning cycle which results must take both elements into account. In this way computer tasks which are seen to be appropriate for enhancing learning in a particular curriculum area and at a specific stage in the children's school experience can be put into place when required. This necessitates the following conditions:

- sufficient hardware (computers and printers) must be available;
- an appropriate and adequate supply of software must be available;
- the teachers must be familiar with the software and the ways in which it can be used to best effect;
- the timetable must permit sustained access to the machines;
- the children must have the necessary, prerequisite experience to undertake the computer tasks allotted to them.

Curriculum mapping and schemes of work

Looking at the curriculum element of Figure 6.1, much ICT is now expected to be taught through subject-focused activities, so ICT must be planned to match the programmes of study in each of the subject areas. At the same time the overall experience of each of the children must be coherent, so that they build on their previous experiences and develop further skills as they move up the school using a suitable range of software. This mapping of ICT to subject or topic areas and across the years provides the whole school framework for ICT use, around which detailed schemes of work can be developed. For all schools there are a number of common elements to be considered and guidance materials and 'skeleton' schemes are readily available. Many are devised and published by government agencies and IT teaching associations. The QCA (Qualifications and Curriculum Authority)/ DfEE *Exemplar Scheme of Work* (1998), which is sent out to all schools, needs mention here. It gives quite detailed suggestions for learning objectives, possible teaching activities and expected learning outcomes for 28 different units covering the six primary years for all IT programmes of study. The links to subjects are given in suggested integrated tasks. Other schemes are also available on the Internet, and further advisory materials taking different approaches are likely to be published through the Virtual Teachers' Centre (see the appendix for details). Having collected all the information from their own ICT audit, schools could review the published frameworks, considering whether one or other of these might be helpful to them in their specific situation.

In devising their own ICT schemes of work schools can elect to take one of two approaches to mapping ICT across the curriculum and across the years: the toolbox approach or vertical and horizontal tracking.

The toolbox approach
This approach starts with the IT requirements as outlined in the National Curriculum and from these prescribes an essential 'kit' of software to be used by each year group. This ensures that the minimum requirements for the children's experience are met, without overburdening teachers with the need to continually learn a range of new programmes. Typically, in Years R, 1 and 2, the kit will contain:

- a simple graphics (painting) program;
- a simple word processor;
- a data handling package;
- A Roamer or simple Logo package;
- an adventure game or small problem-solving games.

More software would be introduced progressively throughout Key Stage 2.

This approach offers a manageable starting point for schools where the staff have little ICT experience. However, it suffers from the implicit notion that ICT is an add-on to the curriculum subjects rather than an integral part of them. The focus on software may also bring with it an unwanted emphasis on *techniques* rather than *processes* (see Chapter 3). It is really important that teachers taking this approach ensure that ICT activities do not become divorced from other classroom activities by linking them directly to specific curriculum subjects. The children understand and interact with ICT techniques and processes because they have goals of their own to achieve: they need to use both a word processor and an art package, for example, to create the story book they are producing in English exactly as they have imagined it.

Vertical and horizontal tracking

When the ICT strands of communicating/handling information and modelling/control form the vertical dimension of the planning matrix then the curriculum requirements of the subjects themselves constitute the horizontal components. Figure 6.2 shows the outline for this. The grid can be completed by inserting the

	Applications	Communicating and handling information	Controlling and modelling
English		Use a template and word bank to plan a story	
Maths	Discuss remote control toys		Roamer journeys
Science			
History			Arrange My World screen on period houses
Geography			
Art			
Design and Technology			
RE			

Figure 6.2   Vertical and horizontal tracking

names of computer programs or activities in the relevant sections. This can be done broadly first of all for overall whole school coverage and then gradually refined for different age groups or individual years; a few detailed suggestions for a Year 1/2 class can already be seen in Figure 6.2. From this framework particular ICT software applications such as interrogating a database can be explicitly detailed, and staff can consider the following questions: do we have suitable software to use in each subject area and each age band? Do we need to plan the purchase of new items for next year? If so what are our priorities?

The next development is the production of schemes of work for each year. These detail ways in which the software will be used, the time required for using it (given the proposed computer availability), and the appropriate part of the year for the work to be carried out. When these have been elaborated all the ICT requirements for each year can be integrated into a single diagram to produce a *computer use plan* for the year. This can be checked for feasibility in terms of deployment of resources and time. The final check can be made across all the years to ensure ICT capability is being developed.

This approach locates ICT experiences more firmly within the curriculum ensuring an integrated experience for pupils and a clearly delineated approach for teachers. Vertical and horizontal tracking from the curriculum starting point feeds back to resource management and helps to determine the logistics of computer and software allocation between classes. As well as highlighting the need for new equipment or software, it also focuses on staff development needs, led by curriculum requirements. In particular, plans must be made to ensure that teachers are confident and happy with their approach to the teaching of ICT within the subject areas as mapped out in the framework document. Cameo 3 touches on this issue. The next consideration is the vital role which the teachers have in ensuring that whole school planning is completed and implemented.

The teacher

Professional development and ICT

Whenever new software is acquired the staff need time, access to computers which will run the new software, the software itself and the associated backup materials. Training is also necessary to:

- appreciate what the new software offers;
- decide on its possible contribution to the curriculum;
- become familiar with the way it works;
- develop appropriate teaching approaches with it which teachers feel are suitable for the learning needs of children in their class.

Throughout this book we have stressed the centrality of the class teacher's role to the creation of worthwhile learning opportunities within the classroom setting. We have also indicated that to have a truly effective impact, some agreements need to be reached between colleagues about how to integrate the good practices of individuals into a coherent and cohesive whole. Class teachers need to work together, in subject groupings or age phase teams, to formulate a view about the way in which their individual planning makes a contribution to the achievement of the identified school and year group aims for ICT. They each need to ensure that the opportunities offered to the children within the various areas of the curriculum actually support the continuity of their learning through the appropriate use of ICT.

For this to be successful teachers require time set aside for their own development – learning time which it is easy to underestimate. Upitis *et al.* (1997) suggest there are three stages which one passes through in developing competence in any area. If we think of these stages in relation to ICT and teachers' competence we can picture something like this:

1 *The compliance phase*: teachers are sufficiently familiar with the software to be able to use it as demonstrated, perhaps using the support materials provided by the trainer or manufacturer.
2 *The cognizance phase*: teachers can begin to make the software 'their own' as they develop their appreciation of it and use it in slightly different contexts with a variety of approaches.
3 *The creative phase*: teachers are able 'to drop all the supports' they have used so far and to use the software entirely to meet their own teaching objectives, often in ways never dreamt of by the software developer!

Within any school there are likely to be colleagues at different stages in their ICT use of particular software applications. As they all need to deliver the curriculum to their various classes, planning together and sharing resources can provide great strength and confidence. All the advantages of group work apply to teachers too!

Learning to use ICT is not a single one-off experience. It is a continual cycle of personal development. Short courses – always favoured because they are cheap to provide – are probably of greater use to experienced computer users who can, through a one-day course, for instance, quickly come to appreciate the facilities within a new piece of software and to recognize the potential it offers in education. The experienced user can then spend time after the course getting to know the program better and deciding on an appropriate teaching approach for it; a self-development process which may easily take ten times longer than the original course and prove difficult without a personal computer.

For a novice user one-day courses can seem challenging. It is easy to become overawed by all the possibilities being offered without feeling able to get into a position of being able to use any of them confidently. The experience may be more off-putting than encouraging. If novice users are first provided with personal computers and then supported in a computer culture in which they are empowered as users then courses like this will be more successful. On long external courses this build-up is part of the process (Finlayson and Perry 1995) but it could also be developed over the period of a year or more through a well thought-out in-school induction programme. The ICT coordinator is a key figure in such an approach but sympathetic colleagues are also vital in offering personal support.

The design and implementation of such in-school training is the responsibility of the senior management team, and they must make the resources – both time and personal computers – available for teachers if they are to upgrade their skills. The costs may appear high, but the return on such an investment will be very real and worthwhile, producing teachers who are competent, confident and creative personal users of ICT, able to share these abilities with their pupils.

Summary

In this chapter we have looked at some of the whole school issues which impinge on teachers in classrooms trying to make effective use of ICT. The school issues considered have involved:

- resource allocation to ensure that all children have sufficient access to computers to support their learning and develop their ICT competence;
- whole school planning of ICT in the curriculum to give children a progressive and coherent experience of ICT throughout their schooling;
- investment in teacher development as an ongoing process, to ensure that all staff have competence with, and appreciation of the educational approach with ICT applications to put the planning into practice.

Other issues, such as the role of the ICT coordinator and school management require a book to themselves!

Points to consider

1 How important do you think home computers are for children's education? Are you aware of:

- which pupils have them?
- the purposes for which they are being used (e.g. games playing, Internet searches);
- which software children regularly use at home?
- how often they use specific programmes?

Develop a pro forma to show children's out-of-school computer experiences.

2 In order to pass on as much information on children's ICT experience as possible as they move up the school the children could be asked to write to next year's teacher about what their achievements in ICT this year have been, outlining what they enjoyed most about specific applications or processes they have learned.

3 A useful approach for sharing information about ICT use within classrooms is to plan a schedule of activities in which each staff member presents details of one application which went well in their own teaching including some samples of children's work.

4 Many schools have their own web pages now; if you have not seen them you could go through the Virtual Teachers' Centre or other web sites for schools on-line. (See appendix for details about how to access the Virtual Teachers' Centre.)

Conclusion

To make predictions about the future impact of ICT on education seems to tempt fate to prove you rapidly wrong. All we would want to say is that we feel rapid change will continue to be characteristic of this area as cheaper, faster, more flexible and versatile commercially required ICT equipment increasingly becomes available for teachers to consider using in their teaching. The ways teachers find to utilize such equipment will no doubt change with every innovatory step. Teachers' primary role will, however, remain that of maximizing children's learning, but the ways in which this is achieved will evolve as ICT develops.

Our final, ideal cameo would show teachers and learners working together confidently and efficiently to access information, when they really need it, by means of a wide range of technological support mechanisms. They would demonstrate by their actions and discussions that they know where the information they need is to be found, how it is organized, how to assess its quality and utility for their purposes, and most importantly of all, when this knowledge will make them more effective as learners.

We would wish this book to encourage teachers to retain their key role as 'mediators' in learning processes involving ICT, ensuring active participation and partnership between learners, teachers, the curriculum and ICT itself.

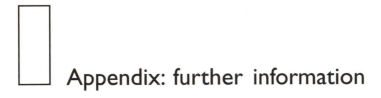

Appendix: further information

Chapter 1

Early literacy programs

There are a number of phonics programs for children relating letter sounds to words using an *A* for *Apple* association approach. Animated Alphabet and Letterland are two of these. They do not make use of computer sound facilities. Talking word processors offer more than this and can be set to create letter sounds as keys are pressed and to read complete words. CD-Roms are available with full sound facilities and a variety of presentations or games relating symbols to sounds for both letters and words. There are also many versions of 'talking stories' some of which will explain the meanings of words for bilingual children.

Laptops in early literacy

The references to laptops in early writing and play scenarios are taken from a project the authors carried out with schools and nurseries in Derby City. This was part of the laptops project sponsored by NCET.

Chapter 2

Simulations and adventure games

Adventure games present children with imaginary worlds where they are asked to help to solve a major problem. Sometimes they are allocated specific roles, particular powers and responsibilities. Adventure games are a form of simulation where children play the role of villagers, police or civic authorities involved with decision making from different points of view. Simulations of this type involve children in researching, practical investigations and seeking information from other sources. Adventures can also involve extensive imaginary work relating to most areas of the curriculum. They offer a central classroom theme for a number of weeks. For more about adventure games see Whitebread (1997) or Chapter 6 in Wegerif and Scrimshaw (1997).

Chapter 3

Information retrieval

NCET have produced a number of useful publications about searching and retrieving information from the Internet or CD-Roms. These are available from BECTa and include: *Making Sense of Information* (NCET 1995c); *Information Skills in the National Curriculum* (NCET 1996); and *Finding Out: Using Reference Material on CD-Rom* (NCET 1997a).

Art with ICT

Some interesting discussion material on the role of ICT in art and art education is given in the following articles:

McGowan, J. (1997) Can design software make a useful contribution to the art curriculum? The experience of one school, in B. Somekh and N. Davis (eds) *Using Information Technology Effectively in Teaching and Learning*. London: Routledge.
Michie, D. and Johnston, R. (1988) A metaphor upside down, in A. Jones and P. Scrimshaw (eds) *Computers in Education 5–13*. Milton Keynes: Open University Press.
Scrimshaw, P. (1988) Computers in art education: threat or promise? in A. Jones and P. Scrimshaw (eds) *Computers in Education 5–13*. Milton Keynes: Open University Press.

Integrated learning systems

These are computer applications used particularly for basic numeracy and literacy, but do not meet National Curriculum requirements as IT applications. These requirements imply a certain degree of pupil autonomy in the choice and use of applications where appropriate across the curriculum. This means that although the ILS computers are exceedingly expensive – particularly for primary-school budgets – other computer systems to run the Internet, CDs, word processing, data handling and control are also required. Schools considering taking the ILS route should carefully consider all the available evidence on the potential learning gains, and the conditions underlying those gains before committing themselves. If children were given the same amount of access to computers running other programs that they require for successful ILS use (a minimum of three 20-minute sessions per week) they might also show high learning gains here!

Using texts within word processors

The curriculum IT support materials for history, produced by NCET, give exemplar materials for developing historical reasoning through text analysis using word processors, suitable for Key Stages 2–3. Both these and the data handling packs provide examples and techniques which could easily be adapted for Key Stage 2 pupils, and for other curriculum areas. The materials are available from BECTa. Two good examples are *Improving Students' Writing in History Using Word Processing* (1997); *Searching for Patterns in the Past Using Spreadsheets and Databases* (1998).

Chapter 4

Logo programming and turtle graphics

Turtle graphics is part of the full Logo programming language, which can be used like any other programming language (Basic, Pascal etc.) for building up applications. In turtle graphics a small pointer (the 'turtle') moves around the screen drawing a trail behind it in relation to body-centred commands – that is, movement forwards or to the left or right. Some examples of commands are:

forward 10	go forward 10 steps;
right 90	turn on the spot to your right (in a clockwise direction) through 90 degrees;
repeat 4 [forward 100 left 90]	carry out the two commands to move forwards and turn through 90 degrees to the left four times, thus completing a square.

Turtle graphics is used in mathematics to develop sequencing and logical thinking, hypothesizing and testing, and to develop mathematical ideas related to patterns in shape and number, mathematical abstractions and generalizations.

Drawing regular polygons provides numerical patterns which relate to spatial patterns. Thus there is a halving and doubling pattern to drawing squares and octagons, or triangles and hexagons:

repeat 4 [forward 100 left 90]
repeat 8 [forward 100 left 45]
repeat 6 [forward 100 left 60]
repeat 12 [forward 100 left 30]

4 sides (a square);
8 sides (an octagon);
6 sides (a hexagon);
12 sides (a dodecagon).

Circles are the limiting case of regular polygons, having a theoretically infinite number of sides. In practice within turtle graphics anything with more than 20 sides tends to look circular, depending on the resolution of the screen.

Procedures
Most versions of Logo have about 130 'primitive' commands such as *forward, back, repeat, print, clearscreen*, etc. Any number of new commands, called 'procedures' can be built from these, and new names created for each. The above commands to draw a square could be made into a procedure and given the name 'smallsquare' by typing in:

```
to smallsquare
repeat 4 [forward 50 right 90]
end
```

Now a square can be drawn by typing the procedure name.

A procedure for a square of any size can also be built by changing the forward input (which is 50 units in *smallsquare*) into a variable, which can again be given an arbitrary name, in this case 'size':

```
to square :size
repeat 4 [forward :size right 90]
end
```

Procedures allow very complex pictures and patterns to be drawn using procedures within procedures. They also provide the basic commands for control technology (see below).

Floor turtles
Turtle graphics can also be carried out by three-dimensional robots which move around on the floor, controlled from the computer through an infra-red connection, or by free-standing battery operated models which incorporate their own control panel. They can carry out all the same actions as the screen turtle, and may also carry a pen to trace their route. 'Roamer' and 'Pip' are two such battery operated floor turtles. They are useful in helping children to develop ideas of control commands, as an introduction to early number work, and to Logo programming.

Roamer is programmed through buttons on its surface. If a new command is entered it is added onto the sequence of commands already in its memory and when GO is pressed it carries out the whole sequence. To start a new routine the memory must be cleared by pressing the 'CM' button twice. A limited number of procedures can also be built, given numbers rather than names (i.e. P1 = Procedure 1).

Pip is programmed in a similar manner but has a different appearance, being square and black. Both Pip and Roamer can be dressed up to play other roles in imaginative play settings which give purpose to their journeys.

Logo and control
An area not touched on in this book is that of control – a required part of the National Curriculum for IT. Turtle graphics provides an introduction to this area, suitable for Key Stage 1, but at Key Stage 2 children develop models of houses, traffic lights etc. with control elements incorporated. Lights, motors and buzzers are activated from the computer through a control box. Light, position and magnetic sensors can also be detected through the same interface. The commands used to programme the sensors are all Logo procedures, so an understanding of procedure-building through turtle graphics forms a sound basis on which to develop these control applications.

Chapter 5

My World

The concept of a My World screen is very simple: it consists of a background with objects which can be freely arranged on it. The objects may be movable, copyable or text. A movable object is picked up and dropped with single mouse clicks and moved with the mouse. It can be placed anywhere on the screen or thrown away in the bin. Copyable objects give rise to new identical movable ones with each mouse click, so the entire screen can be filled with one small copyable object. Text can either exist on the screen as a movable or copyable object, or be created by the user from a little text pad. Children generally delight in throwing things away in the bin!

There is usually no 'right answer' in My World tasks, though matching tasks may be developed with words to match pictures, or numerals to match collections of small items, and the finished screen can be printed out. The work is 'open-ended' and can be approached in any way.

Structured databases

Essentially, databases used in primary schools are simple electronic versions of card index systems, such as used to be found in libraries

or police record files. These are flat file structures, not the more complex relational databases which are not used at primary level. The
file used in Cameo 3 is made up of identically structured *records*, one
for each butterfly or moth. Each record has a set of *field* headings
such as wingspan, size, colour, food of the caterpillar etc. with the
specific data for that insect. Some data is *numeric*, as in size and wingspan, where other entries are words (*text* or *alphanumeric*), as in colour
and food. Some data may also be entered as a choice of several fixed
options.

It is quite common for software producers to also sell data files, for
use on their databases, which match particular topics in the National
Curriculum. Some history, science and geography topics particularly
lend themselves to this approach. Pupils can then use the files to find
out particular information, or to search for patterns and relationships in
the data, to deepen their understanding of the topic.

The search facility in a typical database program relies on matching
the data entry within a particular field. To do this requires the children
to instruct the computer in particular ways. For example, when working
with text data, a match may be sought by using terms such as *the same
as*, or *includes*, and adding a particular word. With numerical data the
search terms can be *equal to, greater than* or *less than* a particular value, so
to find the butterflies and moths with the largest wingspan a search
could be done as:

search;
field – wingspan;
greater than 45 mm

The problem the pupils had in the cameo was in thinking of a suitable
value to be *greater than*, for which they needed to know the range of
possible sizes.

The *graph* facility typically allows histograms (block graphs) or pie
charts to be drawn showing frequency data. The wingspan values would
be grouped into six or nine equal categories, and the block graph would
represent the number of insects in each category. It would also give the
size range for each block.

The *sort* facility will allow the records to be sorted on any chosen
field, alphabetically for text fields and numerically, with a choice of
smallest first or largest first, for numerical fields.

More information on ways of using data handling within history, science and design technology are given in the following NCET packs,
available from BECTa: *Enhancing Science with IT* (1995); *IT in D&T: The
Modelling Pack* (1996); *Searching for Patterns in the Past Using Spreadsheets
and Databases* (NCET 1997c).

Discussions on classroom use of data handling tools are given in:

Smith, H. M. (1997) Do electronic databases enable children to engage in information processing? in B. Somekh and N. Davis (eds) *Using Information Technology Effectively in Teaching and Learning*. London: Routledge.

Ross, A. (1988) How does information retrieval help children's learning? in A. Jones and P. Scrimshaw (eds) *Computers in Education 5–13*. Milton Keynes: Open University Press.

Chapter 6

Concept keyboards and word banks

A concept keyboard is essentially a flat array of 128 programmable touch sensitive 'switches' or keys arranged in an A3 or more usually A4 size 16 x 8 block. Each key, or block of keys (commonly 4 × 2 or 4 × 4) is programmed to have the same effect as a particular combination of normal keys. This programming is then represented on a paper overlay placed on top of the keys with pictures, words or other symbols in the appropriate positions. Used with a word processor each block of 4, 8 or 16 keys would be programmed for a particular word, phrase or sentence. A single press on that block would then enter the whole word, phrase, or sentence onto the screen.

This alternative concept keyboard approach can be used with any number of different applications (turtle graphics, for example) but has had the greatest impact as a simple approach to word processing, particularly when used by children with reading difficulties. Here the flexibility of the overlay, being able to use pictures as well as words, is important. Sixteen words or phrases can be comfortably set up on an overlay, but far fewer or indeed far more can be used. Children need to be able to find the words they want and to recognize them, so there is a trade-off between the number of words and the ease of finding them. The concept keyboard does not stop the normal qwerty keyboard from operating but works alongside it, so only the difficult or less common words need to be put on the overlay while the well-known ones are keyed in using individual letters.

The teacher's expertise is needed in deciding the words required for particular groups of children for specific writing tasks. Programming the computer for each overlay takes less time than drawing the layout on paper, with a bit of practice, and once the overlay is created it can be saved and recalled for use at any time. Some schools have developed banks of concept keyboard overlays for particular subjects or topics which are then used by several different teachers as they require them. Differentiation of a writing task can be automatically built in by designing overlays at different levels of difficulty. For some children all the required words can be provided, with or without pictures, to give hints of the meaning, where for others just the most difficult or specific topic-related words can be used, leaving them to enter most of their text via the normal keyboard.

Another particular advantage of concept keyboards is for group work and discussion with children where they have to make decisions between them. The concept keyboard, particularly in A3 size offers a common focus which is more accessible to any group member than the normal keyboard.

Microscope, the journal of the Micros in Primary Education Group has over the years provided many good examples of concept keyboard use and supplied software and overlays together with suggestions for teachers and reports by classroom users.

On-screen word banks

Word banks fulfil the same function as concept keyboards, but on the screen itself within word processors. They provide whole words or phrases which can be directly entered into the text. The word bank may be an integral facility of a particular word processor, or an additional program designed to be run in conjunction with any word processor ('Clicker' on Acorn or PC machines operates like this). Word banks occupy a separate window, to one side of or below the main text window of the word processor. On-screen word banks are much easier to set up for most purposes than concept keyboards, but lack the flexibility of the paper overlay. Some word banks will allow pictures to be used with them, but at this point the advantages of ease-of-setting-up tend to be lost. However, if the word bank includes speech facilities, which is now quite common, then for most uses this more than compensates for the loss of pictures.

Internet information for schools

The Internet is an area of rapid growth and development with many sites of use to teachers and school planners, as well as to parents and children. A list of relevant sites immediately becomes dated! However some pointers can be given to sites which are likely to remain for some time.

The BECTa home page address is http://www.becta.org.uk. Through BECTa you can get into a great many useful educational ICT sites, including those concerned with curriculum IT support (CITS) materials and publications, as mentioned earlier. Information is also available about the Internet itself in a 14-page free information sheet which gives an overview of what it can do for education, guidance on accessing it, advice on censorship issues and reference sources and contacts for help in getting started. This can be printed off from the Internet, or can be obtained directly from BECTa at Milburn Hill Road, Science Park, Coventry, CV4 7JJ.

The National Grid for Learning, through which the Virtual Teachers' Centre is accessed, can be found at: http://www.ngfl.gov.uk. Other education centres include: Education Online (http://www.edon.org.uk); Edu-Web (Research Machines Teachers' Centre – http://www.eduweb.co.uk); Ultralab (learning resource centre at Anglia Polytechnic University – http://www.ultralab.anglia.ac.uk).

Government information on education can usually be found via the DfEE site at: http://www.dfee.gov.uk. The Ofsted site, including a searchable database of Ofsted reports, can be found at: http://www.ofsted.gov.uk/ofsted.htm.

Finally, the *Times Educational Supplement*, Internet edition, including a searchable archive of articles published in the last five years is located at: http://tes.co.uk.

Bibliography

Baddeley, G. (ed.) (undated, circa 1992) *Learning Together Through Talk: Key Stage 1 and Key Stage 2*, National Curriculum Council and National Oracy Project. London: Hodder & Stoughton.

Bennett, N. (1994) Managing learning in the primary classroom, in J. Bourne (ed.) *Thinking Through Primary Practice*. London: Routledge.

Boaler, J. (1993) Encouraging the transfer of 'school' mathematics to the 'real world' through the integration of process and content, context and culture, *Educational Studies in Mathematics*, 25: 341–73.

Boys, R. (1997) The Weston Rhyn fax fairies, *Microsope – Early Years Special*, MAPE and Newman and Westhill College, pp. 26–8.

Brown, J. and Underwood, J. (1997) *ILS: Potential into Practice*. Oxford: Heinemann.

Bruce, T. (1996) Celebration of play. TACTYC conference presentation, Greenwich, November.

Bruner, J. (1983) *Child's Talk*. Oxford: Oxford University Press.

Cambourne, B. (1986) Rediscovering natural literacy learning: old wine in new bottles, in R. Stoessinger (ed.) *Using Language Learning Conditions in Mathematics*, PEN Papers 68. NSW, Australia: Primary English Teaching Association.

Carpenter, B. (1995) Building an inclusive curriculum, in J. Ashcroft and D. Palacio (eds) *The Primary Teacher's Guide to the New National Curriculum*. Brighton: Falmer Press.

Case, R. (1985) *Intellectual Development: Birth to Adulthood*. New York: Academic Press.

Chadwick, A. (1995) Teddy bears' literary bonanza. Presentation given at the Laptops in Early Literacy Seminar, University of Derby, June.

Cook, D. (1998) 'Sense making, play, and emergent mathematics', unpublished PhD thesis. University of Derby.

Cox, M. (1997) *The Effects of Information Technology on Students' Motivation: Final Report*. London: King's College/NCET.

Crook, C. (1987) Computers in the classroom, in J.C. Rutkowska and C. Crook (eds) *Computers, Cognition and Development*. New York: John Wiley.

Crook, C. (1994) *Computers and the Collaborative Experience of Learning*. London: Routledge.

Daniels, H. (1996) (ed.) *An Introduction to Vygotsky*. London and New York: Routledge.

Davis, N. (1998) A virtual community of teachers. Paper presented at Learning, Quality and the Information Age conference, Homerton College, Cambridge, March.

Dawes, L. (1997) Teaching talking, in R. Wegerif and P. Scrimshaw (eds) *Computers and Talk in the Primary Classroom*. Clevedon: Multilingual Matters Ltd.

DfE (Department for Education) (1995) *The National Curriculum for England and Wales*. London: HMSO.

DfEE (Department for Education and Employment) (1997) *Excellence in Schools*. London: HMSO.

Donaldson, M. (1978) *Children's Minds*. London: Fontana.

Downes, T. (1996) The computer as a toy and tool in the home: implications for schools and teachers, *Education and Information Technologies*, 1: 191–201.

Downes, T. (1998) Using the computer at home, in M. Monteith (ed.) *IT for Learning Enhancement*. Exeter: Intellect Books.

Dunne, E. and Bennett, N. (1990) *Talking and Learning in Groups*. London: Macmillan.

Edwards, D. and Mercer, N. (1987) *Common Knowledge: The Development of Understanding in the Classroom*. London: Methuen.

Engestrom, Y. (1996) *Non socolae sed vitae discimus*: towards overcoming the encapsulation of school leaning, in H. Daniels (ed.) *An Introduction to Vygotsky*. London and New York: Routledge.

Ernest, P. (1990) *The Philosophy of Mathematics Education*. Brighton: Falmer Press.

Farish, D. (1989) Computer as catalyst, *Talk: The Journal of the National Oracy Project*, 2: 17–19.

Ferrera, R.A., Brown, A.L. and Campione, J.C. (1986) Children's learning and transfer of inductive reasoning rules: studies of proximal development, *Child Development*, 57 (1): 87–99.

Finlayson, H. (1985) 'The development of mathematical thinking through Logo programming in primary school children', unpublished dissertation. University of Edinburgh.

Finlayson, H. and Cook, D. (1998) The value of passive software in young children's collaborative work, in M. Monteith (ed.) *IT for Learning Enhancement*. Exeter: Intellect Books.

Finlayson, H. and Perry, A. (1995) Turning sceptics into missionaries: the case for compulsory information technology courses, *Journal of Information Technology for Teacher Education*, 4 (3): 351–61.

Fisher, E. (1997) Educationally important types of children's talk, in R. Wegerif and P. Scrimshaw (eds) *Computers and Talk in the Primary Classroom*. Clevedon: Multilingual Matters Ltd.

Forman, E.A. and McPhail, J. (1993) Vygotskian perspective on children's collaborative problem-solving activities, in E.A. Forman, N. Minick and C.A. Stone (eds) *Contexts for Learning*. Oxford: Oxford University Press.

Forrestal, P. (1992) Structuring the learning experience, in K. Norman (ed.) *Thinking Voices*. Sevenoaks: Hodder & Stoughton.

Goldstein, G. (1997) *Information Technology in English Schools: A Commentary on Inspection Findings 1995–6*. Coventry: Ofsted in conjunction with NCET.

Hall, N. (1987) *The Emergence of Literacy*. London: Hodder & Stoughton.

Hartland, S. (1998) The Dudley Internet project, in *Computers Don't Bite Teachers*. London: BBC Books.

Heath, S.B. (1983) *Ways with Words*. Cambridge, U.K.: Cambridge University Press.

Hess, R. and McGarvey, L. (1987) School-relevant effects of educational uses of microcomputers in kindergarten classrooms and homes, *Journal of Educational Computer Research*, 3: 269–87.

Higgins, C. (1995) Information technology, in J. Ashcroft and D. Palacio (eds) *The Primary Teacher's Guide to the New National Curriculum*. Brighton: Falmer Press.

Hoyles, C. (1988) *Girls and Computers*. Bedford Way Papers 34. London: Institute of Education.

Hoyles, C. and Sutherland, R. (1989) *Logo Mathematics in the Classroom*. London: Routledge.

Hughes, M. (1986) *Children and Number: Difficulties in Learning Mathematics*. Oxford: Basil Blackwell.

Jessel, J. and Hurst, V. (1997) Children exploring the queen's house in hypertext: has the hype any educational potential? in B. Somek and N. Davis (eds) *Using Information Technology Effectively in Teaching and Learning*. London: Routledge.

Kress, G. (1997) *Before Writing: Rethinking the Paths to Literacy*. London: Routledge.

Labbo, L.D. (1996) A semiotic analysis of young children's symbol making in a classroom computer centre, *Reading Research Quarterly*, 51 (1): 356–85.

Langer, E.J. (1997) *The Power of Mindful Learning*. Harlow: Addison Wesley.

Lankshear, C. (1997) *Changing Literacies*. Buckingham: Open University Press.

Light, P. (1993) Collaborative learning with computers, in P. Scrimshaw (ed.) *Language, Classrooms and Computers*. London: Routledge.

Lynch, O. (1998) Learning quality and the information age. Keynote address at the Learning, Quality and the Information Age conference, Homerton College, Cambridge, March.

Merry, R. (1998) *Successful Children, Successful Teaching*. Buckingham: Open University Press.

Miller, L., DeJean, J. and Olson, J. (1997) Lessons from the classroom: integrating CD-Rom talking books into the curriculum. Paper presented at CAL conference, Exeter, April.

Moll, L.C. and Whitmore, K.F. (1993) Vygotsky in classroom practice: moving from individual transmission to social transaction, in E.A. Forman, N. Minick and C.A. Stone (eds) *Contexts for Learning*. Oxford: Oxford University Press.

Moyles, J. (1989) *Just Playing?* Milton Keynes: Open University Press.

Neate, B. (1991) *Finding Out About Finding Out*. Sevenoaks: Hodder & Stoughton.

NCET (1993) *Access to Words and Images*. Coventry: NCET.

NCET (1995) *Differentiation: Taking IT Forward*. Coventry: NCET.

NCET (1995c) *Making Sense of Information*. Coventry: NCET.

NCET (1996) *Information Skills in the National Curriculum*. Coventry: NCET.

NCET (1997a) *Finding Out: Using Reference Material on CD-ROM*. Coventry: NCET.

NCET (1997b) *Improving Students' Writing in History Using Word Processing*. Coventry: NCET.

NCET (1997c) *Searching for Patterns in the Past Using Spreadsheets and Databases*. Coventry: NCET.

Nicolopoulou, A. and Cole, M. (1993) Generation and transmission of shared knowledge in the culture of collaborative learning: the fifth dimension, its play-world, and its institutional contexts, in E.A. Forman, N. Minick and C.A. Stone (eds) *Contexts for Learning*. Oxford: Oxford University Press.

Phillips, T. and Scrimshaw, P. (1997) Talk round adventure games, in R. Wegerif and P. Scrimshaw (eds) *Computers and Talk in the Primary Classroom*. Clevedon: Multilingual Matters Ltd.

Pollard, A., Broadfoot, C., Croll, P., Osborn, M. and Abbott, D. (1994) *Changing English Primary Schools: The impact of the Education Reform Act at Key Stage One*. London: Cassell.

Pratt, D. (1995) Young children's active and passive graphing, *Journal of Computer Assisted Learning*, 11: 157–69.

QCA/DfEE (1998) *Exemplar Scheme of Work for Information Technology*. London: QCA.

Reid, J., Forrestal, P. and Cook, J. (1989) *Small Group Learning in the Classroom*. Scarborough, WA: Chalkface Press.

Sanger, J. (1997) *Young Children, Videos and Computer Games: Issues for Parents and Teachers.* London: Falmer.

Schaffer, H.R. (1996) Joint involvement episodes as contexts for development, in H. Daniels (ed.) *An Introduction to Vygotsky.* London: Routledge.

School Curriculum and Assessment Authority (SCAA) (1997) *Expectations in Information Technology at Key Stages 1 and 2.* London: SCAA.

Scoresby, K. (1996) The effects of electronic storybook animations on third graders' story recall, unpublished doctoral dissertation. Brigham Young University, Salt Lake City, UT.

Shade, D. and Watson, J. (1987) Microworlds, mother teaching behaviour, and concept formation in the very young child, *Early Childhood Development and Care*, 28: 97–113.

Sinclair, J. (1983) Young children's acquisition of language and understanding of mathematics, in M. Zweng, T. Green, J. Kilpatrick, H. Pollack and M.S. Suydam (eds) *Proceedings of the Fourth International Congress on Mathematical Education.* Boston, MA: Birkhauser.

Sparrow, L. (1991) The airport as one world, in N. Hall and L. Abbott (eds) *Play and the National Curriculum.* Sevenoaks: Hodder & Stoughton.

Tagg, B. (ed.) (1995) *Developing a Whole School IT Policy.* London: Pitman Publishing.

Tharpe, R. (1993) Institutional and social context of educational practice and reform, in W.A. Forman, N. Minick and C.A. Stone (eds) (1993) *Contexts for Learning.* Oxford: Oxford University Press.

Underwood, G. and Underwood, J. (1997) Children's interaction and learning outcomes with interactive books. Paper presented at CAL conference, Exeter, April.

Underwood, G., McCaffrey, M. and Underwood, J. (1990) Gender differences in a co-operative computer-based language task, *Educational Research*, 32: 44–9.

Underwood, J. (1998) Making groups work, in M. Monteith (ed.) *IT for Learning Enhancement.* Exeter: Intellect Books.

Underwood, J., Cavendish, S., Dowling, S., Fogelman, K. and Lawson, T. (1995) Are integrated learning systems effective learning support tools? Paper presented at CAL 95 conference, Cambridge, March.

Upitis, R., Phillips, E. and Higginson, W. (1997) *Creative Mathematics.* London and New York: Routledge.

Vaughan, G. (1997) Number education for very young children: can IT change the nature of early years mathematics education? in B. Somekh and N. Davis (eds) *Using Information Technology Effectively in Teaching and Learning.* London: Routledge.

Vygotsky, L.S. (1978) *Mind in Society.* Cambridge, MA: Harvard University Press.

Wegerif, R. and Scrimshaw, P. (eds) (1997) *Computers and Talk in the Primary Classroom.* Clevedon: Multilingual Matters Ltd.

Wendon, L. (undated) *Letterland Software*. Cambridge: Barton.

West, A., Hailes, J. and Sammons, P. (1997) Children's attitudes to the National Curriculum at Key Stage 1. *British Educational Research Journal*, 23 (5): 597–613.

Whitebread, D. (1997) Developing children's problem solving: the educational uses of adventure games, in A. McFarlane (ed.) *Information Technology and Authentic Learning*. London and New York: Routledge.

Wood, D. (1988) *How Children Think and Learn*. Oxford: Blackwell.

Wood, D.J., Bruner, J.S. and Ross, G. (1976) The role of tutoring in problem solving, *Journal of Child Psychology and Psychiatry*, 17: 89–100.

Woods, P. and Jeffrey, B. (1996) *Teachable Moments: The Art of Teaching in Primary Schools*. Buckingham: Open University Press.

Wray, D. and Medwell, J. (1989) Using desktop publishing to develop literacy, *Reading*, 23 (2): 62–9.

Index

Page references to figures appear in *italic* print.